Poetry

8-2023 Bristol

PITY THE DRAGON

pity the dragon

POEMS ON CHINESE THEMES BY BRETT RUTHERFORD

THE POET'S PRESS
Pittsburgh, PA

Copyright © 2023 by Brett Rutherford
All Rights Reserved

Version 1.3

This is the 309th publication of
THE POET'S PRESS
2209 Murray Avenue #3
Pittsburgh, PA 15217-2338
www.poetspress.org

POEMS ON CHINESE THEMES
    The Thirteen Scorpions   13
    Bai Hu, The White Tiger   20
    On a Chinese Fan by Dong Gao   29
    The Orphaned Vase   31
    Old Scholar Under Autumn Trees   34
    Mrs. Wang's Rebellion   35
    Pity the Dragon   37
    The Loft on Fourteenth Street   39
    Two Scholars Atop A Cliff   46
    Things I Never Dreamt I'd Eat   48
    Chinatown, 1975   50
    Figures on a Kangxi Vase   52
    Les Ancients Buvant   57
    The Azaleas of Ningpo   63
    The Tea-Pet Toad   65
    October Storm   67

KANGXI DRINKS TEA FROM HIS EGGSHELL PORCELAIN TEACUPS
    First Lunar Month   69
    Second Lunar Month   71
    Third Lunar Month   72
    Fourth Lunar Month   73
    Fifth Lunar Month   75
    Sixth Lunar Month   76
    Seventh Lunar Month   77
    Eighth Lunar Month   79
    Ninth Lunar Month   80
    Tenth Lunar Month   81
    Eleventh Lunar Month   83
    Twelfth Lunar Month   84
    Epilogue   86

EMPEROR LI YU, A LIFE IN POEMS

TO THE READER   89

AT THE COURT OF SOUTHERN TANG
  Pretending to Be A Fisherman   93
  Autumn Day-Dreams   95
  Choosing No One   96
  Awakening in Early Autumn   99
  Dancing on Autumn Leaves   102
  Making Spring Happen   105
  The Floating Things   107
  Woman of Spring   110
  Making Love to the Empress   112
  Sweeping the Tombs   114
  Down South   116
  The Forbidden Palace   118
  Visiting the Dowager   121
  The Other Woman   124
  The Empress, Alone   126
  The Prisoner   129
  Waiting for Her   131
  The Hut   132
  The Beloved Speaks   135
  The Interruption   136
  Alone in the Temple   140
  The Court Officials   142
  Doubts   145
  The Futile Bouquet   148
  Long Is the Sadness   151
  Nightmare   152

PRISONER OF THE SONG EMPEROR
   Meditation in Exile   157
   Night Sounds   161
   Monotony   163
   Ninth Day of the Ninth Month   165
   The Parasol Trees   167
   Separated   171
   The Land of Wine   173
   Tears   176
   Horses As Fierce As Flying Dragons   177
   Lichen   179
   Am I Awake?   182
   Places and Names   185
   Of Trysts Gone By   186
   Empty Is the Past   187
   What Kind of Poet?   189
   Written While Dying   191

ABOUT THE POEMS   195

ABOUT THIS BOOK   203

ABOUT THE AUTHOR   204

POEMS ON CHINESE THEMES

THE THIRTEEN SCORPIONS

A Monologue of The Emperor Qianlong (1711-1799)

I bid you welcome
    to the Summer Palace,
to this, my garden
    behind the Hall of Paintings,
and now that you,
    Father of the Jesuits,
have learned enough Chinese
    to dine in my presence,
we shall dispense with bowing,
    kowtowing, and the like.

We can speak now,
    man-to-man,
though it best be said
    as god to man
for unlike your god
    who is infinitely
    receding, I am here.

I am the Son of Heaven.
For as long as I can recall
I was the Son of Heaven.
Father and Grandfather
Yongzheng and Kangxi
thought themselves so,
but they were merely
openers of the way;
they conquered and pacified,
thrust Manchu virtue
into the soft Han underside,
gave steel
where only bamboo
had sufficed.

Truly, I am the most
interesting person
who has ever lived
(or so the eunuchs
daily remind me).
I have composed,
or signed my name to
some forty thousand
poems; well-schooled
in martial arts,
I could break a man
in two, bare-handed.

I hunt. The deer tremble.
I make war. Unruly tribes
flee back to their borders.
My name and seal
are on ten thousand vases.
My visage has been painted
by European as well as Han.
My armies have gone as far
as Lhasa, whose Dalai Lama
bows to me —
               What's that?
Disaster in Burma? Vietnam
refusing to bend the knee?
You are impertinent, Holy Father —
time will tell — but here,
the servants come with tea,
dainties and dumplings.
Let us leave politics, and speak
of other things. You know,
I have learned to speak Tibetan,
and their Yellow Church priests
shall be in charge of my tomb
when Heaven takes me.

But tell me true, Jesuit Father,
how just as Manchu conquered Han
yet all of China has ravished me
with art and music and poetry
so that I scarcely have time for war,
does not your little god pall
before the sight of our mountains,
the mists on the Yellow River?

You eat like a Chinaman. I see
the way you eye that eunuch
(I will send him 'round
with the rest of the dumplings
if that pleases you? It does?)

Is China not
the world's true center? Not Rome!
Although I ban your faith
and god, and god's wife, and son,
and those ever-bleeding saints
are not permitted here — you stay.

You collect our pottery,
Tang, Song, Yuan, and Ming.
Calligraphy eludes you
and yet two hundred scrolls
of painted landscapes
have found their way
into the Jesuit dwelling.
Does China not always win,
like a great concubine,
by merely standing by in beauty?

Now, walk this way with me —
hand me the cricket jar,
Old Chen! — and we shall see
in this otherwise barren

rock garden, one standing stone.
gongshi, we call these —
how weathered and worn
and full of cavities it is!

Step up to the boundary
of crushed cinnabar
and look close! They come!
They come! Cringe not,
for the thirteen scorpions
are bound to the stone
and the gravel around it.
It is their universe.

Wonder you may
how I have ruled
for sixty years; how none
have raised a hand against me
and succeeded.

One duke, one general,
one martial-arts fanatic,
two who called themselves
my brothers and blood-princes,
four who put up banners
and called me usurper:
see how they scurry
away from my shadow!
Emirs and khans and kings,
four I did not behead or slice
now wriggle here and rip
at another's bodies
with fangs and venom'd tails.

The one on top? You know
I had three empresses, consorts
fifteen, and half a dozen
concubines. Only one was bad,

and there she basks. Nothing
would please her more than progeny.

A concubine
the only female on an island
with twelve male reprobates.
They will have nothing
     to do with her. Ironic, no?

They will go on this way
forever, so long
as my hand feeds them
now and then.
Watch, as I lift this jar
that contains their dinner,
as I rattle the lid
just ever so slightly,
like cats they come running.

Step back — the cinnabar
line is poison to them
and they cannot pass it.

Old Chen, come hold
the Jesuit Father up.
He seems a little dizzy.
Is your taste too fine
to witness thirteen scorpions
fight over and eat
a solitary cricket?
It is only an insect.
It is their favorite food.

The dumplings, perhaps,
have made you sleepy.
Rest on this garden seat.
Is this not like
the place you call Purgatory,

where evil-doers reside
on a mount of their iniquities?

Just such a thing, in miniature,
a Daoist master made for me.

Come, take a look
as I uncover the victim.
What say you? Empty?
Why so it is.
Look deeper, Father
of the foreign devils' god.
Slough off your priestly
robes, your cross and jewelry.
Do you not feel the change?
Catch him, old Chen!

I am the Son of Heaven.
I have always been
the Son of Heaven.
I am the most interesting man
who has ever lived.

And you —
    whom I hold
    in my hand and toss
    into the hungry horde —
you
are a cricket.

BAI HU, THE WHITE TIGER

1
I dreamt — it was no dream! —
for there, on the floor, the melted snow,
the window-lattice broken, night coals
from the brazier scattered everywhere.
I dreamt he was there beside me:

the great white cat, tiger of Siberia,
lord of Manchurian wastelands. He,
my servant comes trembling to tell me,
has taken up residence
at the far end of the north pavilion.

"Ah! let him stay! Bring me my sword?
No! my pen and scroll! I must wash
my thoughts with a draught of tea.
Renew the fire. Refill the *yi xing*
pot with pale white tea leaves."

"He is Death," my servant tells me.
"Bai Hu, the White Tiger,
has roamed these hills for half
a thousand years. He has no mate;
they say he is Hunger incarnate.
With fire and gong and beaten shields
we can drive him away forever."

I shake my head and answer:
"Bai Hu is welcome here, Old Chen.
He is Autumn, the world's Fall,
my autumn, the end of my youth.

Where he treads, frost follows,
his breath the snow that fells the wheat
and makes the maples scream
red murder. Long have I known
he would be my guest one day."

"Cover the window," old Chen admonishes.
He shudders as a chill breeze enters
and the willows begin shivering.
"I will send for torchmen to light your way,
an escort of our bravest youths."

Already I see two feline eyes alight.
They grow larger in the passageway.
"It is too late. A guest once past the threshold
must be offered food and lodging.
The tiger may come and go as he pleases."

I point to where the great beast enters.
My servant issues a piercing cry.
Ignoring us, the monster, white
in the whiter moonlight, lies down
on the warm tiles of the coal hearth.

I return to my calligraphy.
"You see, Old Chen, how he reclines.
I do not think he means to harm me."
Chen bows and backs to the doorway,
and as he closes the double door, calls back,
"Bai Hu no longer hunts by night, but
tomorrow brings terror to the countryside.

The tiger will kill the fallow deer,
and, should you venture forth by daylight,
he, pretending not to know you,
will turn on you as well. Your kindness
will all too soon be forgotten. An old poet
is sweet fruit after a venison banquet."

2
Oh night of nights for Tiger and Poet!
'Twixt Venus and Jupiter, one moon
hangs crescent; 'twixt sleep and dawn
the great beast cradles me, and I, him;
sword, fang, and claw forgotten, defying
our double death; a frozen interval,
two hearts abeat, and four lungs breathing.
I dream of being a great beast, rampant;
the tiger dreams of the calligraphy brush,
the tail-flick ink flow that places songs
on paper, words in the ears
of unborn readers and listeners.
I taste the blood in his mouth, the flex
of great legs that can overleap all prey;
he tastes pale tea and delicate sauces,
the savor of rare wine in a heated bowl.

3
My guest is gone when I awaken.
As dawn breaks through,
the Heaven-tree, the willow boughs,
the distant pines sigh, shiver, shrug:
they will fight for a green day,
bird-harboring, leaf-tipped
to the lambent sunbeams.
Somewhere, out there, the tiger
drags Fall behind him as he hunts
life down with a panther frenzy.
Great clouds of birds assemble and flee
before him; cave, den, and warren
pull in their denizens for the long sleep
of winter. He leaves a trail
of antlered skeletons, doe-widows,
trees clawed clean of summer.

4
My place is here with lamp and teapot.
I write a poem. I roll and seal
the rice-paper scroll, wipe clean
the brush and close the ink-jar.
This is not just any autumn's beast.
There is some cause for which
he spares me; he is not my Autumn
nor the death-breath of my last winter.
I have ink enough for a thousand more poems.

No, Bai Hu is the Tiger of Entropy:
he drags tornados, kill-winds
and glaciers behind him.
He would blink out
the world's great cities if he could;
he would strike down the moon
as his ball-of-string plaything,
leave earth an orphan
in a sunless cosmos.

If I let him.

Tomorrow, while he sleeps,
wherever he sleeps —
    and I see the place,
    in the shade of the pines
    beyond the placid river —
I shall send Chen for my finest mount,
my armor and my banner men.
I shall ride forth,
my flag the Three-No poem of summer
defiance: No to death,
No to surrender, No to the idea
that all things must have their autumn.

5
At the second dawn, we set forth
on our fastest ponies.
I have sixty-one years
as I leave the pavilion.
I have fifty-one years as I cross
the great wheat fields.
I have forty-one years
as I track the maple-red forest.
I have thirty-one years
as I ford the river,
horse-neck and saddle
just barely above the water.
I have twenty-one years
as Old Chen passes to me
the great halberd
of my ancestors.

Now, I shall kill the White Tiger.

— 2010, rev. 2011

ON A CHINESE FAN BY DONG GAO

Hand-painted, a universe of greens and grays
emerging from a background mist
on the sewn strips of a Chinese fan[1]:
the scholar, a man of some wealth
and even greater erudition, has brought
(o wonder of labor and engineering)
a good half dozen scholar's stones,

each high as a house wall, soft stone
eroded to honeycomb by a millennium
of patient rain and hollowing,
forming three sides around his table;

at ease with his calligraphy, the brazier
bright and burning with water a-boil,
the servant refilling the *yi xing*[2] pot
as fast as he drinks down
the finest of water-nymph teas;

the reedy crooning of an *er-hu*[3]
fiddle at his right; off to the rear
a *pi-pa*[4] lute player awaiting
her turn to please him, the rocks
a perfect amphitheater;

birds hovering, pruned trunks
of trees on one side bending
the trunk in an artful curve

---

[1] *Chinese fan.* Painted by Dong Gao (1740-1818). The Chinese fan described here was sold at Christie's in 2009.
[2] *Yi xing.* A red-purple clay used for making scholars' teapots and other ornamental ceramics.
[3] *Er hu.* The two-stringed Chinese fiddle.
[4] *Pi pa.* The Chinese lute.

(how long it took to tease
one cherry in and among
the hollows of the *lingbi*[5] stone!).

No solitary scholar this,
alone in a gazebo perched
on some cliff above the cloud-line:

he has a secondary grove,
o'erhung with pine and willow
beneath whose shade
a table is spread with all his poetry,
where two friends tune the zheng,[6]

to whose melancholy fingerings
(glissando and tremolo)
they'll echo back his lines to him,
even while serving girls unwrap
the afternoon repast of tofu,
pickles piquant with rice vinegar
and red chilis, and red-bean cake.

Other friends ambulate
amid the upthrust rocks
and clinging tree-roots,
catching the drift but not
the meaning of his poems
as wind and waterfall
hum through the sighing pines.

It is a place so beneficent
that in it poems are superfluous —

well, almost.

---

[5] *Ling bi.* Name of the hollowed, perforated stone from Anhui province favored for scholar's stones
[6] *Zheng.* The Chinese zither.

THE ORPHANED VASE

Two decades or more I have studied it:
that double-dragon-handled vase
from my New York hauntings.
Bought from a Chinese store
about to shut down forever,
its unsold vases stacked,
dust-covered orphans
that had never found a home.

Today I regard it with new eyes
and undertake to learn its origins,
and what the wriggling floral shapes
and tangled leaves can tell me.
Amid the leaves are Treasures:
a thick square book in a silken cord,
a checker board awaiting two players,
two rice-paper scrolls tied up

blank for calligraphy to come,
and two rhinoceros horns
predicting happiness
for the vase's owner.

It was intended, no doubt,
to be a young scholar's first vase,
its carmine glaze the blush
of a young man's ardor,
its unknown, ardent flowers
all petals open to the sun.

It is all good omens, but no one came
to the old shop on Mott Street
to carry it off; no scholar sipped
his oolong tea and wrote poems
in the cheer of its good karma.

Close scrutiny reveals
some hint of the reasons why:
one of the dragon handles
is missing the monster's snout.

Some accident — a fall, a ricochet
of a bandit's bullet, broke off
this beast's ability
to snort a blowtorch back
at a would-be attacker.
One also sees
the whole vase is a-tilt.
It leans some five degrees
off vertical, so doomed to sit
like someone whose leg
is shorter than the other,
a tipsy vase just ready
to take a tumble.

It is a century old, I guess.
It is lonely for its maker,
for the fine-haired brush
that painted it, for the wheel
on which it was cast lopsided.

It comes from a kiln
that exists no more. One day,
a Japanese bomber took sight
at the Wude Sheng factory
and all was blown
to smithereens.

Thou, sad vase,
thou, snoutless dragon,
thou, limping, tilted vessel,
orphan of war and history.

OLD SCHOLAR UNDER AUTUMN TREES

*From a Chinese Painting
and Poem by Shen Zhou, 1470 CE.*

Gone, gone, gone. Gone to the west
wind, the leaves have fled. Still, there is
sun, still some shade under half-
disrobed maples. I loosen
my collar, I just lean back
and read my book. No clock, no
appointments, all idleness.
It is a long book; I have
all the Autumn ahead
to read, or to gaze on up
at the sky that pulls on me.
Here below — or on up there —
who knows what I shall do next?

MRS. WANG'S REBELLION

In Chinatown,
Mrs. Wang
mounts
a quiet rebellion
against the ways of the elders.

She has done all
her mother asked her:
married the boy
the matchmaker ordained,
bore sons and daughters
in regular order,
burned joss and incense
at every altar,
sending ghost gold and peaches,
phantom cars and televisions
Hong Kong Hell dollars
to the teeming, greedy dead.

Now her husband travels,
has mistresses, won't talk
about his gambling.
Her children are gone,
married to foreign devils
Her round-eyed grandchildren
won't learn Mandarin,
will never send joss riches
to her when she is dead.

Now she becomes a whirlwind:
She sells her jade and porcelain,
cleans out her savings account,
buys an airline ticket
for San Francisco —
from there, who knows?

She pawns the statuette
of pearly white Kuan-Yin,
the Goddess of Mercy
whose only blessing
was endless childbirth
and washing and ironing.

On a whim she buys another
to take its place at her bedside:
a foot-high Statue of Liberty
with batteries and glowing torch.

She leaves it for her husband,
her wedding ring
on its spiky crown.

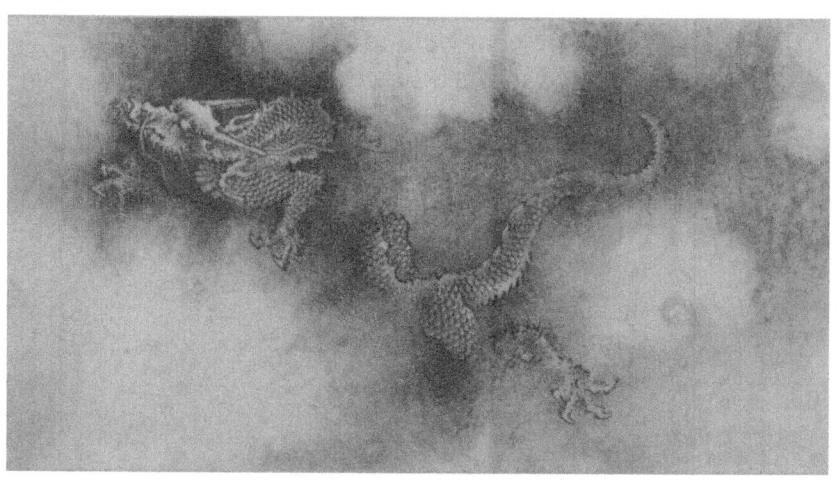

PITY THE DRAGON

Surveying my vases,
teapots and paintings,
I count no less
than thirty dragons
leaping from peak
into a sea of clouds,
ever in chase
of that flaming pearl
it is never allowed
to swallow, apart
from its kind around
the curve of vase,

contending with phoenixes,
cloud clots, and even
perversely huge flowers,
it is never permitted
to meet one of its kind,
to caress, converse,
make love. One wonders
if new dragons are ever made
at all. Seldom entirely

free, one claw behind
a tuft of smoke, the edge
of a cliff-top, the line
of a rooftop — even
the artist constrains it
with such device
in fear of its free flight,
its all-consuming
flame. How free
is free if one is ever
alone and above
the loved world?

THE LOFT ON FOURTEENTH STREET

Doors painted bright,
the tapestries stitched brilliantly,
the singing hall, the dance pavilion —
all ashes now, their incense gone,
their light engulfed in night,
their echoes muffled, silent.
Bring the lute, I will sing.
     Pao Chao, c. 465 CE

Am I the only one who sees it? Up there.
 That third floor loft,
all dark, the one whose windows gape wide
 through every season,
the one whose ghost-white curtains, now grayed
 by soot and tattered
by wind-flap, flutter like flags of abandonment, a place
like a village deserted before a certain onslaught,
bereft even of spider-webs or sunning cats or plants.
Rain, snow or sun — it seems not to matter at all up there.
One wonders why owls or bats or pigeons haven't gone in
to penetrate the darkened space inside, for that at least
would tell me something, while dark panes tipped
 in to darker space
gives only one answer: — a nullity, that no one lives here.
Is that a light? One glow — I can see it as I pass by
slowly on Fourteenth Street —
 a distant yellow bulb somewhere
way back, relentlessly dim and dull, night and day burning.
No matter how long I linger, I've never seen shadow
nor any illumined thing beam back or obscure its glow.
If only some hand, with a wrist and an arm below it
would show itself, reach out to pull the window shut at last.

But it goes on and on, like some tortured modernist art
(blank canvas, untouched piano keys, actors not acting)
the flutter-flash of curtain at wind's beck, the solitary
beam of a single bulb on a tall and shadeless pole lamp.
Am I the only one who knows him? That man. It is his loft.
We met in Central Park — yes, in the shrubbery! — we met
that day he first arrived in America. I was the first
to touch and welcome him, new-found from far-off China.
He spent his first American night on the floor with me.
The bohemian mattress lay next to the printing press.
Cartons were piled everywhere —
    I was leaving New York that week.
I helped him read the street signs, pronounce
    the words he needed
to navigate the days until his funds caught up with him.
We made love until dawn; he slept against me as light shafts
broke day into the concrete canyons and made palaces
of derelict old cast-iron dry-good stores, the dust-mite sun
that every day wakens some special urgent magic.
I envied him the adventure just beginning — my need
was to flee for some months as my printing business folded.
I gave him the key to my soon-to-to-abandoned loft —
"Stay here, I said, until the landlord comes
    to take possession.
You'll have a few days at least.
    If I could take you with me…"
His raven hair intoxicated me, his eyes caught me
with a sense of unpredictable intelligence.

When I came back, our friendship blossomed.
    He was my gateway
to the best of a world that is all but hidden to most.
What feasts we savored in Chinatown! Chen Ma Po Do Fu!
Sea slugs in casserole! Beijing Duck! Dragon and Phoenix!
The *pi-pa*, the *er-hu*, the bright world of Chinese music,
mad whirl of the Monkey King, the death and return to life
of the Butterfly Lovers; the long dark conspiracies
of eunuchs and emperors, flute girls and fierce concubines,

of Empress Wu, and Ci Xi, the last dread Dowager,
seen on the dim movie screens of Chinatown theaters,
even the awful kitsch of The Red Detachment of Women.
One day I played, to his astonishment, "The East Is Red,"
mock-improvised on my harpsichord. His Middle Kingdom
he gifted me, as I brought him to Beethoven, Mahler,
Handel and harpsichords. Happy, our times together!
(But we were never one, despite my always wishing it.)
Manhattan's day-long man-show and its nocturnal orgies
drew him into the world of "always-chasing, never-caught."

Over the years our paths converged, and parted,
    and met again.
My Hudson crossing wedged between us —
    what a foolish thing.
When I moved to my cliff-top dwelling, just minutes away,
his phone calls stopped; he never visited. That Tunnel rose
like an angry dragon between us. I had ceased to be;
a faraway ZIP code denizen, a toll-call outlaw.
Orbiting the same sun, we became like shadow planets
exactly opposite, each to the other invisible.
I heard that his mother had visited, furious with him
for his myriad boyfriends. "I want you married!"
    she shrieked.
"You pick one. Stay with someone. I don't care if it's a man!"

I drifted to Providence, plague-fleeing, driven by Muse
to a new locale in Poe and Lovecraft's haunted footsteps.
Alone, I had continued along my Chinese journey.
Weekends I drifted through Chinatowns —
    tea houses, the cry
and clamor of the opera house enthralling me again —
White Snake, The Golden Brick, The Peony Pavilion! —
museums and galleries and auction houses teaching me
the glory of Chinese painting, the breathless awe I felt
regarding a single porcelain bowl emblazoned with
five peaches in full blush bloom over which, in perfect arcs,
five bats fluttered — perfect long life in perfect happiness.

The Monkey King, the lord of Chaos,
    now graced my mantle.
Kuan-Yu, the lordly general with his golden halberd
guarded my doorway; my wall aflame as Yuan pagodas
perched in impossible perspectives on dream-shrouded hills,
and one great Taoist dragon emerged from a yellow scroll.
This, my house, compounded of so many things
    he showed me.
I found myself back in New York at last, to live and work.
I thought of him often. The gulf of not speaking became
an ocean. There would be no story to this, if this were all.

2

> *Those I have known and loved my lifetime through —*
> *How many can I count? One hand's fingers suffice!*
>   — Po Chü-I, circa 820 CE

Even though I am now an "older man," I'm never drawn
to older men. But here, a cultured gentleman, Chinese
and kindly, a devotee of the arts and the opera,
invited me for dinner and mischief (in one of those
vast beds no doubt constructed for the Forbidden City.)
Some instinct told me, Go with this.
    Some things are meant to be.

As I had only just resumed my old Manhattan haunts,
I thought much about old friends, the lightning jabs
    I'd suffered
while reading so many obits and epitaphs, too soon,
too young, too many, my whole vast web of acquaintances
shattered; thought, too, of the disconnects
    that the years impose
on early friendships. Each one of them seemed
    more precious now
as I began to make, and receive, what I came to call
"the annual endangered species phone call." Always
I thought, there's one I'll see again, that fickle, spoiled, bad,

obsessive and art-loving, music-besotted fellow.
We were not done with each other, and I had come ten times
more into his world since we had spoken last. Where was he?

He was there in the phone book, yet no one answered, ever.
His neatly-typed name was glued above the lobby mailbox.
Each time I passed there now, I entered
    and rang the doorbell.
Always that window was open, always that one dim light
in the far darkness, the curtains like a warlord's banner.
Where was his face, that glance of recognition and greeting?

The dinner was past, the rosewood bed explored in the dark
in various positions. My host and I sat talking,
and he asked me how I came to know so much of China,
its culture and literature, its ways and its secrets.
And so I spoke of my friend, of our seeing Liang Shan Po
and Qiu Ying-Tai, the gender-bending Butterfly Lovers,
of our long but often interrupted friendship, of how
I had been trying in vain to reach him for months. "Perhaps
his mother has died and he's gone off to Taipei. Perhaps
he's made the often-dreamt-of journey to the mainland —"
"What is his name?" my host asked, interrupting me. I spoke
his names — the English one he'd taken,
    and the Chinese one.
His face fell, "I knew him. He came here often.
    His friends, too.
Mad for music. Big stereo. He painted — or tried to."
He paused, lifted his cup of pale oolong. "Six months ago —
about six months ago, he died of AIDS."
    The breath was ripped
from my being. My heart sank; I felt I'd hurtle downward
to the earth's core if someone didn't catch me.
    "I'm sorry —"
he started, and then our eyes met and we realized it —
that we had met so he could tell me this — of all the men,
of all the myriad Chinese men in Gotham, of all

the myriad lonely American men he could have
    invited home.
The message had passed between us
    like a death-white cloud —
a thunder-blasted peach tree and a sky devoid of bats.
Later that night — how could I not? —
    I walked on Fourteenth Street.
The curtains still billowed, the panther eye-beam yellow light
still glowed. His name was still there —
    the rent still paid from afar
by his mother? His things still up there uncollected?
    the paints,
those sketched-and-then-abandoned canvases piled up
    in a heap —
a great, dusty horde of art books and classical music —
or — nothing? a vast, dead space of which that shorn drapery
was but the fringe, a Mongolian waste of unslaked hunger,
a never-relenting sandstorm — and far, far off, a tomb
lined with the terra-cotta likenesses of his lovers?
(Which one was his death? To which of them
    was he Death?) No more!

3

Oh, that I could make the world-globe shrink,
so that suddenly I'd find you back at my side.
              —Wang Chien (830 CE)

Art is the great denier when the artist is silent.
I waited all these years to write this, as though my silence
would cancel his passing, and the maelstrom
    that took him, too.
Perversely, I'd open a phone book and find his name there.
Why? I'd pass those windows, open, the curtains billowing.
Why? A whole year passed. One day the panes
    were pulled shut tightly.
There! A new name, neatly writ and pasted on the mailbox.

You see! He is dead! It is as final as a tombstone,
as final as the phone book, which no longer lists him now.
And more — it is as though he never existed. To me
alone was bountied that first night's touching,
    mine the laughter
of all the days we shared (that never a fraction of all
I was willing to give!). But still I had no tears for him.

Art is the great denier when the artist is silent.
Can world and time erase their errors? Another year passed.
I found myself on that block again. Windows were open!
Perhaps if I rang the doorbell, the new tenant would share
some shred of knowledge about the eccentric prior tenant —

I froze as I stood before the mailbox. The tenant's name,
that new, hand-lettered name had come unglued, it was
gone, fallen off, ripped off, or it had gone *pentimento*
(just as old paintings reveal the older art beneath them),
his name asserting itself, just as his absence ruled here.
I turned and fled, and I did not look up at those windows.

Imagine a life so lightly laid upon the hard world
that all that remains of him is his name, a mere undercoat,
a line on a page in a discarded past year's phone book,
a scratched-out entry in a hundred men's pleasure journals.
Three breaths, his real name on the wind
    (his name unspoken
except in my heart, and in the dream of autumn thunder) —
not in a tomb with white flags fluttering — not burning joss
at his ancestral shrine — but here,
    in this poem, remembered.

TWO SCHOLARS ATOP A CLIFF

Fu Bao Shi paints them:
two scholar friends
who seldom agree
on weighty matters,
friends now
and forever regardless.

One faces the painter.
Perhaps he is glad
to be seen there
facing another cliff
we can only imagine.
The other looks off
into the spiky peaks
whose forested slopes
play hide and seek
in perpetual fog.

Posed at right angles,
neither scholar sees
the same reality;
neither can know
how Fu sees them

seeing. Fu cannot see
what either scholar
perceives.

Black ink,
brown washes.
One nature,
many mountains.
Each man alone
in a universe
of seeing.

THINGS I NEVER DREAMT I'D EAT

Duck feet, sea slugs,
lotus root dry
   from winter mud,
eggs lost and found
inside a clay pot
   a "hundred years,"

baby eels, slimy
   (aphrodisiac?),
tree-bark fungus
afloat in soup,
shark fin, dried
   octopus snack,

Old Pock-Marked
   Mrs. Chen's
tofu (the scholar's
rocket fuel),
mysterious red
sausages, pork
belly, bok choy,
a stinky fruit
(durian) milkshake,
noodles transparent,
tentacular,

the act of faith
that no one you know
has, after a thousand cuts,
wound up inside
today's pork bun —

all these I know,
but I draw the line at
stew of a black dog,
and jellyfish.

CHINATOWN, 1975

Gossip among
young Asian men,
with whom I dine,
   a guest, a stranger,
yet somehow as in
    as they are out.

Outsiders always,
   some seldom stray
   North of Canal Street,
employment limited
to under-the-radar
exploited jobs, unless
the overseas mother,
the rich uncle,
paid one's way
to a good school,
escape into
the melting pot.

Slowly, I learn
the pecking order:

the ABCs
(American-born Chinese),

rich Asians
   on monthly checks
   from anxious parents,
well-off Taiwan
   or Singapore families;

"jump ships," the
mainland arrivals
    from Mao's horrors,
cardless, furtive,
evading questions.

Americans see none of this,
each bowing waiter,
    each unseen worker
in kitchen or sweatshop,
a Charlie Chan cipher.

Outcast among
a colony of outcasts,
I am at home here
at this round table whose
lazy susan rotates
a casserole of friendship.

From here, we head out
for the Chinese opera.

FIGURES ON A KANGXI VASE

The world might end
and they would not know it.
High on the slope
of a sacred mountain,
six mortal scholars gather
in a mansion garden.

Master Liu
has arranged everything
to mitigate
the heat of August.
A folding screen
conceals sun's glare
and shades the table
where four enjoy
cold wine
from an antique flagon.

Hand turns around
blue-figured vase.
Gao, the exiled
high official, arrives
with a banned book
close to his heart.

His nephew, young
and handsome, feels
overdressed, and would
prefer a shady glen
to nap in, hatless
with collar undone.

A small boy, restless,
another bored
participant,
would rather be at
his bow and arrow,
or watching the play
of wild horses, but here
the slow pace of old men
calling to mind a poem,
leafing the pages to find
a Confucian dictum,
must suffice.
Honor it is
to be with the wise.

> *Hand turns around*
> *blue-figured vase.*

Crouching, a servant
adds coals to fire
beneath the brazier
meant to refresh
brown *yi xing* teapots.

Low walls zig-zag
the edge of Liu's estate.
Trees overhang
the painted screen,
branches identical
to what the artist
painted there.
How daring to place
a painted forest
before a real one!

>*Hand turns around*
>*blue-figured vase.*

In mountain fog
the distant peaks,
even the edge
of a nearby precipice
are lost in white
as pale as porcelain.

All is foreground
and an extended hand
might touch cold glaze,
tracing the curve
of the limits of existence.

Frozen this once
and forever, the old men
debate the merits
of poetic styles,
deliberate
on whether things
are permanent
or fade to nothing.

Cool wine, warm tea,
the rise and fall
of a remembered song;
muffled, the dim roar
of falling waters;
calligraphy called up
from nothing to drop
upon a blank page.

*Hand turns around
blue-figured vase.*

A day too hot
for any other purpose.
The world might end
if eyes sought deep
into the denser mist,
a yellow glare,
gnat-flecked, in which
two butterflies hover,
weightless, immobile,
and terrified.

What is this blotch
upon pure whiteness?
The burning sun
craving to show itself?
A distant city
ablaze, invaded?
The exploding scream
of a split atom?

Gao, bring the book to me!
Be quick, my friend!
Find the right page,
the words to read,

the names of gods,
if gods there are,
we need invoke.

Here in the clarity
made plain by tea,
a thousand years
of wisdom adheres.

So long, the afternoons,
so short the nights
of bug-bite August.

Here they are safe,
scholars, nephew,
boy, and servant.

Hand turns around
blue-figured vase.

The old ones are drinking.
They need not fear
the world might end.

[A hand-painted blue-and-white vase depicts scholars in a garden. Behind four seated scholars, a painted, folding screen protects them from sun and wind. The trees painted on the screen are the same as those around them. All is foreground — no distant landscape is visible, as though the scene were surrounded by fog. Under the vase's glaze, a large open area has a slight yellow cast, and the vase painter has drawn little dust-flecks around the edge of the mysterious glow, and placed two butterflies hovering there. What looks like a defect in the color of the clay seems purposeful, and we are asked to explain its cause, and why the scholars seem suspended in the foreground.]

LES ANCIENS BUVANT

Figures sur un Vase du Règne de Kangxi

Si le monde se terminait,
ils ne le sauraient pas.

Haut sur le versant
d'une montagne sacrée,
six érudits mortels
se réunissent
dans le jardin d'un manoir.

Maître Liu a tout arrangé
pour atténuer la chaleur
du mois d'août.

Un paravent dissimule
l'éblouissement du soleil
et ombrage la table,
là où quatre amis
dégustent du vin froid,
que l'hôte verse
d'un drapeau antique.

> *Le vase*
> *décoré de figures bleues*
> *tourne dans ma main.*

Gao, le haut fonctionnaire exilé,
arrive avec un livre interdit
qu'il tient près de son cœur.

Son neveu,
jeune et beau,
est trop habillé.
Il préfère faire une sieste
dans un vallon ombragé,
sans chapeau,
le col ouvert.

Un petit garçon,
un autre participant,
semble submergé
par la chaleur et l'ennui.

Celui-ci préfère jouer
avec son arc
et ses flèches,
ou regarder courir
les chevaux sauvages,

mais ici, le rythme lent
des vieillards rappelant
leurs poèmes,

et feuilletant les pages
pour trouver un dicton
confucéen —
elle doit suffire.
L'honneur c'est
d'être avec les sages.

   Le vase
      décoré de figures bleues
         tourne dans ma main.

Un serviteur se penche
pour ajouter des charbons
à un brasero enflammé.
L'eau est ici
pour les théières brunes
d'argile yi xing.

Les murets
zigzaguent le bord
du domaine de Liu.
Des arbres surplombent
l'écran peint
Leurs branches
sont identiques
à ce que l'artiste
y a peint.

Quelle audace
de placer une forêt peinte
devant une vraie!

   Le vase
      décoré de figures bleues
         tourne dans ma main.

Dans le brouillard
de la montagne,
les sommets lointains,
et même le bord
d'un précipice voisin,
se perdent
dans la blancheur,
pâle comme de la porcelaine.

Tout est au premier plan,
et une main tendue
pourrait toucher la glaçure froide,
traçant la courbe
des limites de l'existence.

Figés une fois
et figés pour toujours,
les vieillards débattent
des mérites
des styles poétiques.

Ils délibèrent
sur la question de savoir
si les objets sont permanents
ou s'ils s'effacent
vers le néant.

Vin frais,
thé chaud,
la montée et la chute des tons
d'une chanson mémorable;
étouffé,
le faible rugissement
des eaux qui tombent

Calligraphie appelée de rien
pour tomber
sur une page blanche.

Le vase
  décoré de figures bleues
    tourne dans ma main.

La journée est trop chaude
pour toute autre diversion.
Le monde se terminerait
si les yeux cherchaient
profondément
dans la brume plus dense.

Il y a un éblouissement jaune,
moucheté de moucherons.
Deux papillons y planent.
Ils sont en apesanteur,
immobiles
et terrifiés.

Quelle est cette tache
sur la blancheur pure?
Est-ce le soleil brûlant
qui a envie de se montrer? —
une ville lointaine
en feu, envahie? —
le cri
qui explose
d'un atome fendu?

Gao, apportez-moi le livre!
Soyez rapide,
mon amie.
Trouvez la bonne page,
trouvez les mots à lire,

trouvez les noms
des dieux —
si les dieux existent —
que nous devons invoquer.

Ici,
dans la clarté du thé,
mille ans de sagesse
adhèrent.

Si longues sont les après-midis,
si courtes sont les nuits
d'août,
rongées par les insectes.

Ici,
ils sont tous en sécurité:
érudits, neveu,
garçon et serviteur.

*Le vase
décoré de figures bleues
tourne dans ma main.*

Les Anciens buvant.
Ils n'ont pas à craindre
la fin du monde.

[Un vase peint à la main en bleu et blanc représente des érudits dans un Jardin. Derrière quatre érudits assis, un paravent peint les protège du soleil et du vent. Les arbres peints à l'écran sont les mêmes que ceux qui les entourent. Tout est au premier plan – aucun paysage lointain n'est visible, comme si la scène était entourée de brouillard. Sous la glaçure du vase, un grand espace ouvert a une légère fonte jaune, et le peintre de vase a dessiné de petites taches de poussière autour du bord de la lueur mystérieuse, et a placé deux papillons qui y planent. Ce qui ressemble à un défaut de couleur de l'argile semble intentionnel, et on nous demande d'expliquer sa cause, et pourquoi les savants semblent suspendus au premier plan.]

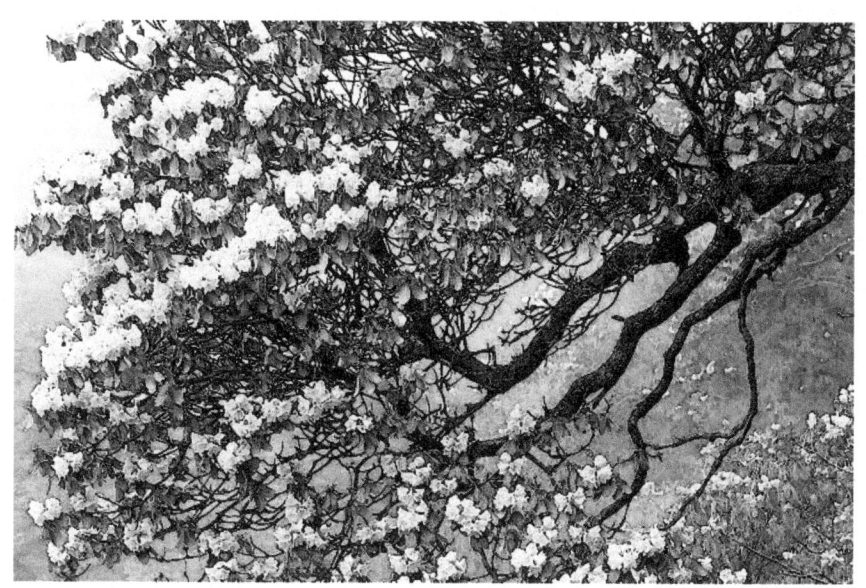

THE AZALEAS OF NINGPO

Legendary and lethal,
the azaleas of Ningpo
cover the hillside, a blaze
of color intoxication.

Goats roaming there,
chewing the blossoms
and leaves, fall down
into a stupor.

A black vase
topped with a burst
of red azaleas,
pink hearts
of rhododendrons:
a death-warning.

A medicine as like
to kill as cure,
used sparingly;

a tiger face
not seen amid
the shrubbery;

fox-fairy perfume,
the fatal allure
of a woman met
by the road-side;

the pain, in exile,
of thinking of home.

Beware the azalea!

** This poem cites several Chinese names for the azalea: "thinking of home," "goat-stupefying flower," and "tiger flower."

THE TEA-PET TOAD

The carved red toad,
mouth open just enough
to hold a single dime,
is a harbinger of wealth,
slow-earned, a tenth
of a dollar doled
out a thousand
thousand times,

the kind of fortune
earned only
by making, by hand,
ten thousand dumplings.

The poor batrachian,
I did not notice
until yesterday,
has only two legs,
a bit of tail

for a tripod
solidity. What of
his other legs?

Ah, that is no tail:
it is a third leg,
tucked under!
For lack of dimes
did he sell
the fourth one off
to a street vendor
whose frog-leg dainties
please the crowd?

That string of coins
slung over his shoulder
implies he should not be
that desperate.

His gem eyes glitter
a greedy ruby and say,
"No need for legs.
I need not leap at all.
Coins come to me,
and pale tea pours
from the heavens
to pool around me."

Serene as Buddha,
wrinkled as sage,
squat on his *I Ching*
pedestal, King Toad
rules the tea table.

OCTOBER STORM

First night of the tenth month
a roaring storm hits town:
thunder from every side,
flash after cataclysmic flash
of blue-white lightning.
Transformers hum
and tempt the storm-stab,
birds hunch in branches,
cats dash
from one dry porch to another.
A set of solitary car-lights passes,
distorted in sheets of rain,
tail-lights at the corner
like the haunted eyes
    of a carnivore

    who has just learned
       he is the last of his kind.
A siren signals a distant fire.

Lightning comes closer,
closest I have known in years.
I open the window,
smell of ozone,
watch as a nearby tree goes down,
raked by the fingernails
of a coal-black thunderhead.

I hold the new jade stone
on which a Chinese artisan
has carved my nascent Mandarin name:

Meng for the dream, the world in which
    all poets dwell —
Qiu for the autumn, my chosen province
    and capital —
Lei for the thunder of the mountain-striding storm.

I am the Dream of Autumn Thunder,
and this storm has called my name,
marked the day of my arrival
in the mysterious Middle Kingdom.

                     — October 1998, Weehawken, NJ.

EMPEROR KANGXI DRINKS TEA FROM HIS EGGSHELL PORCELAIN TEACUPS

FIRST LUNAR MONTH

Snow comes, but so too,
the early blossoms,
plum, while down below
the delicate narcissus
buds up among the
bamboo, indestructible.
My sheltered courtyard
encourages such early
arrivals, out of season.

Nature, I ask,
or sly gardening?

Even when all is still,
fragrance moves on its own
from branch to ground,
along the cold rocks,
and then inside
to the teacup's rim.

Emperor KangXi, Age 45, 1699 CE

SECOND LUNAR MONTH

Evening rain pelts
the abundant flowers
on the apricot trees.

Their stamens radiate
attentive tendrils alert
to every falling drop.
Sunshine or mist
paint watercolor
upon the pale hue
of the white petals.

Am I smelling them,
or does the rain wear
a subtle perfume,
enchanting, seducing
me to put down the teacup,
disrobe, and walk
in the gentle downpour?

THIRD LUNAR MONTH

Peach blossoms should really
employ a whole orchestra
to boom out good news
with their coming.

In Heaven, the peaches bloom
and bear fruit at the same time,
the food the monkeys covet
which makes the gods immortal.

Peach blossoms should fall
with gongs and drums,
alerting the farmers
to renew their labors,
and calling back
the welcome song-birds.

To drink tea beneath
a grove of tall and blossoming
peaches, requires company.
An emperor-to-be
invites two heroes
to drink and swear oaths
of eternal brotherhood.

The peach is the witness
to their youth and honor.

FOURTH LUNAR MONTH

One must be up at dawn
to see the sly peony
untighten its grasp
on night, and drink
the dew of the immortals.

Once it has opened in full,
one almost faints
at how it makes a sphere
of petals a rose would die
to emulate, how ants
come climbing up the stems
to do it worship.

Only the finest
and most intricate
scholar's stone
is worthy to stand
beside the peony,
a sculpture carved
by wind and water,
carried from afar
to be one peony tree's
shade, shelter, and
companion.

An emperor seeks
one such, among
his counselors.
The maddening scent
mocks those who work
in the Jade Hall, where
wisdom is sought.
In vain.

FIFTH LUNAR MONTH

Heavy as rocks
the pomegranates hang
from their sturdy tree.
Yellow spheres aburst
with wet red seeds,
will ripen and blush
at their own abundance.

Their silhouettes,
as I drink tea,
wave back and forth
on the white-washed wall
behind me. The seeds
as plentiful as bees
in a hive, cannot
be counted. Taste
pomegranate, and tea
is, for a moment,
forgotten. It is
the garden's concubine.

SIXTH LUNAR MONTH

Look down below!
Who notices, in mud,
the lowly lotus root
like unearthed jade?
Yet when it bursts to bloom
the whole world worships it.

Two mandarin ducks
swim in the pond.
Their adoration
of the lotus flower
is in the way small waves
make furrows out
beneath their feet,
the small bows
of bill to water.

Only the crane,
from its cloud-perch
can see the symmetry
of lotus, water, shore,
the two brown ducks,
and one aged and lanky
Emperor, cup in hand.

SEVENTH LUNAR MONTH

I sit. I have my tea.
All wish me well,
or so they say.
A seventh cup
they place before me.
Pale tea moves
second-hand as water
boils, goes through
the *yi xing* teapot
(mine alone),
and into the eggshell
porcelain. No hand
but mine has touched it.
All wish me well,
but there is always poison
to worry about.
Mistrust of doctors, too,
if any of them
have better friends,
and younger,
than my Imperial self.

This cup is adorned
with the most reliable
flower: the rose.
Although its heady
oil, perfume's bounty,
makes me sneeze,

I respect its tenacity.
Outliving winters,
indifferent gardeners,
and even dark
conspiracies,

one shade against
another, fratricide,

it just keeps going on.
Just as this emperor
goes on from year to year,
outliving all prophecies,

the tough rose
blooms any time
it pleases.

EIGHTH LUNAR MONTH

Just as the hare
has many progeny,
the *guihua* tree,
osmanthus, from
the far-off Himalayas,

flowers and branches
endlessly, spring,
winter, and fall.
An evergreen,
and fragrant too,
it flavors a tea
and an autumn wine
the Emperor is known
to savor in private.

Two things at least,
the world shall never
run out of: rabbits
and *guihua* trees.

NINTH LUNAR MONTH

O Chrysanthemum,
the only way
to enjoy you,
is with a wine-cup
in hand. Oh, very well,

the Emperor may hold
his favored tea-cup full
of tea made from dried
chrysanthemum petals,

while everyone else
goes mad with its liquor.
Nature joins in.
Insane butterflies
flutter about, bees faint
with overdose of pollen.

Two hands, two eyes
are not enough
to paint the things
chrysanthemums
make happen.
A thousand year's memories
crowd into one day
of sun-burst petals.

TENTH LUNAR MONTH

Indoors,
among the orchids,
the Emperor takes tea,
on the day of many
bloomings. Stubborn,
the pampered ladies
withhold their colors,
refuse to unfurl
their sumptuous hoods.

Unlike the concubines
who come when summoned,
the orchids, kept close
and treasured just as much
as ladies of high families,

cling to rock and branch,
shy and particular.
And then, one day,
the eunuchs come running:

They are ready, Majesty,
the orchids are blooming!

Emperor KangXi in full court robes.

ELEVENTH LUNAR MONTH

Unable to sleep,
the Emperor walks,
unseen,
and unaccompanied
by guard or eunuch
in a sheltered garden.

Is that Narcissus
he sees in moonlight,
breaking the soil
like waves against a dike?
Will they bloom so soon?
Dare they? Is this
the Daoist gardener's
laboratory, where plants
are made to bloom at will,
a fox-fairy's paradise?

At sudden turn, he sees
the old gardener, lamp
in hand, who, horrified
to find his master
walking nocturnal,
trembles and begins
the humbling know-tow.
"Stand, you old magician,"
the Emperor intones.
"You have not seen me.
I was not here. Those were not
flowers seen too soon.

"I have had entirely
too much tea."

TWELFTH LUNAR MONTH

Out and about
when he should not have been,
the Emperor paces
in a poorly-heated room,
hands cupping
the small tea-cup
as much for warmth
as for the taking
of such a small dose
of reality.

His feet trampled frost.
His eyes took in
the beauteous pattern
of ice on flagstones,
the tendril'd snow
at grass's edge.

The sun had risen.
The abundant blossoms
of wintersweet lit up
with the morning's own
gold. Not a leaf
in sight, but all those
waxy petals sprung
from out bare branches.
How rare among
the flowering trees
was this, which bloomed
defiantly
while others shivered,
barren, for warmer days.

EPILOGUE

Twelve cups,
in a rosewood cabinet,
each for a lunar month.
On delicate eggshell
porcelain, so thin
that light shines through,
an artist painted such scenes,
and a poet described them,
calligraphy beneath the glaze.

The cup was for
one drinker only. He,
the Son of Heaven,
ate all his meals alone,
drank tea alone —
not from the coarse cups
seen at the state banquets —
from these small, footed,
porcelain bowls.

With the rising of each moon,
one cup was taken
discreetly away
and replaced with the next.

Emperor Li Yu, a Life in Poems

Adaptations & Expansions from the Ancient Chinese

*For those who led me
into the Middle Kingdom.*

TO THE READER

After almost two hundred years of glory and accomplishments, the great Tang Dynasty of China collapsed in 907 CE. The culture of Tang lingered on in the Southern Tang kingdom, however, ruled by three generations of the Li family. In Southern Tang, the grand traditions of art, music, poetry, and painting thrived, and Buddhism flourished.

Li Yu, the last ruler of Southern Tang, did not inherit his father's military inclinations, and when he assumed the throne at a young age, the realm was shrinking as provinces were ripped away by rival states, the most rapacious of which was the new Song dynasty. Tributes, gifts, and hostages made the tension between Southern Tang and Song more and more fraught with peril.

A poet, dreamer, and pacifist, Li Yu was totally unsuited to rule in a time when China was being split into "Five Dynasties and Ten Kingdoms." Isolated in his palace compound, he devoted himself to writing poetry, and enjoyed not only the favors of his Empress and concubines, but also entered into a scandalous love affair with his wife's younger sister.

Li Yu invited poets and artists from all the war-torn states to Southern Tang, where he housed them as honored guests in their own palace of the arts. More and more Buddhist temples and monasteries dotted the landscape.

The following poem cycle relates the tragic fate of Li Yu, his Empress, and the "other woman," the kind of royal soap opera that fascinates because the outcome is the end of an entire nation. Only 39 poems of Li Yu survive, and every word of them has been woven into this narrative cycle. They are regarded as among the saddest and most emotional poems written in China, and they are sad because this poet, who had everything a mortal could wish for, lost it all.

Captured by the Song army after the siege of Nanjing, Li Yu became a state prisoner, shown off and ridiculed as a former king and would-be emperor. When his new poems offended the Song Emperor, he was ordered to drink poison.

AT THE COURT
OF SOUTHERN TANG

PRETENDING TO BE A FISHERMAN

From Li Yu, Poems 1 & 2

1
My bark is but a leaf,
no oar
but the will
of the errant spring breeze,
this way, that way.

A loose line of fishing string,
on its end a light hook
might serve as rope
and anchor.

The destination:
that flower-covered islet.
The prize:
an icy cask of wine.

Since nothing here is what it is,
but what it stands for,
one or ten thousand waves,
one or ten thousand realms,
what do they matter?

I do not need the island.
I do not, at the moment, crave
the plum green savor of wine,

for I have my freedom.

2
Water, the chemist says,
is incompressible.

The delicate waves,
invisible and relentless,
a unity, break up
a thousand-piled layer
of warlike snowflakes.
They never stood a chance.

Now comes the onslaught:
cloud upon cloud upon cloud
of plum and peach and cherry,
banner-men from Spring's
inevitable and drumless army,
throw themselves down
upon the snowbanks.

White mists enshroud
the waiting wine cask.
I sit with fishing rod and line.

One season has fought and won,
one season has held, and died.
I am doing nothing. This boat
is in a lake that was made for me,
the lake in my own valley
between two hills on which
I have identical pavilions.

Who else
could be as happy as I am?

AUTUMN DAY-DREAMS

From Li Yu, Poem 3

When, of an afternoon, I nap
before my tea at four o' clock,
I dream of forests further south
where Fall lights up the hills;

of yellow, brown bands a thousand miles
long, a vast brush-stroke across
the rivers and mountain gorges;
of all the red of maples touched by frost.

Night falls.
Among the reeds, a boat
abandoned, sits idle,
with drooping sail,
and from above,
a figure barely seen
lifts up his flute
on a moon-crowned terrace,

a song for no one
in particular.

CHOOSING NO ONE

From Li Yu, Poem 4

The ladies have spent all evening preparing.
Just after the bath, the flesh
of consorts and concubines is white
as snow, with here and there
the blush of peach or cherry.

They all line up in the Spring Palace.
It is all for my benefit.
The phoenix flutes trill plaintively,
to make them long for me,
and me, for them,
water and cloud apart
yet yearning to touch.

As they retire, to await
decision and summoning,
the Rainbow-Dress song
goes the rounds, and fades
as the musicians stop
before each chamber.

Which one has overdone it
and fills the air with the scent
of her alluring powder?
Which one thinks
she has found a love-charm?
The aroma of their desire,
compounded by chemists
with thousand-year perfumes,
is enough to make me dizzy.

In my dark pavilion, I tap
the balustrade. Sometimes I just
pick a number; there are so many!

But then I choose: I tell
the servants to light no lanterns,
to let the red candles flutter out.

The wind is up. My horse
is in high spirits. Tonight
I will ride, and we
shall tread the moonbeams!

AWAKENING IN EARLY AUTUMN

From Li Yu, Poem 5

As my eyes open,
    the morning moon,
    pale crescent, sets.
Ashes remain;
    the incense smoke is gone.
Cold, too, the coals
    beneath the brazier —
I must wait for my tea.

Calling no one, I rest
    on this pillow and that,
remembering —

Who was I with? What
    was her name?
No matter! Right now
I have a craving
    for the scent of hay.

  Listen!
Off in the sky somewhere,
    swans weakly call.

Above me,
    on the lattice-work
    of cherry, the orioles
      hungry, unsatisfied,
dart off to fuller branches.

Chrysanthemums, those
    drooping dowagers,
        fade and fall.
No one is up. Later,
these garden embarrassments
will vanish, be sure!

Red maple leaves
    and desiccated petals
litter the enameled floor
    and clog the courtyard.

Sweet autumn carpet,
    crispèd and melancholy:
I shall have it left unswept.

I want to watch what
    the feet of dancers
        do to them.

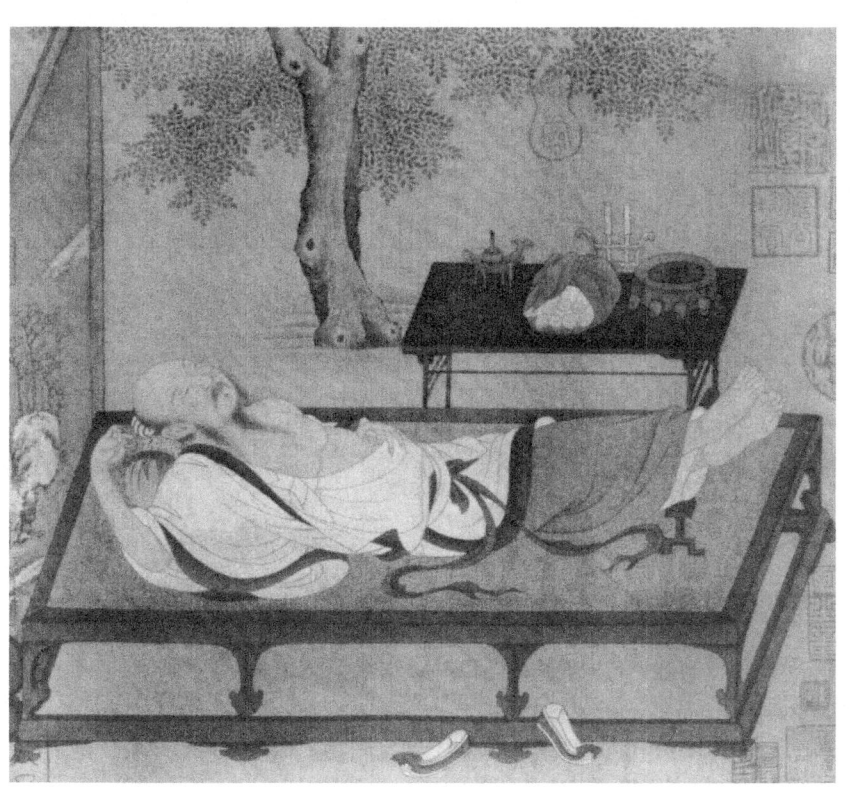

DANCING ON AUTUMN LEAVES

After Li Yu, Poem 6

She has come, as I bid her,
to the unruly pavilion
where leaves and fallen petals
carpet her footsteps.

The sun is but three hours up
but still the Lovely One arrives,
a row of sleepy dancers
behind her,
suppressing laughter
as they move to no music,
but to the breeze itself,
the sway of pine branches.

I clap my hands.
She is a little drunk
from last night's merriment.
Her golden hairpin falls
and another must bow
to sweep it up for her.
Not quite so sure
of this step or that,
no tile or square to guide her,

she pretends to smell
an untouched flower,
    and just as well,
    as it is withered.
Fumbling, she tries again,
the wrong foot forward,

while I delight to hear
small feet unsure of step,
on autumn leaves arranged
by Master Wind.

Somewhere a flute and drum
strike up in another palace
(some being called
to early breakfast!)
Not for me, these sounds!
Shuffle, crackle,
slide, and spin,
whirl, little slippers, my
pantomimes of whim!

MAKING SPRING HAPPEN

After Li Yu, Poem 7

The sound of the little goat-skin drum
makes me want to write poetry.

Fools wait for the falling blossoms
before they say that Spring has come.
To find Spring, you must go early
and walk to the fields in search.
To love a flower that has bloomed
already, is to miss the flowering.

My love presents my favorite cup
with a supple hand. I see
no thumb. The blue-glazed
porcelain surrounds
an inner whiteness, a wine
so pure it has no color.

Is Spring delayed
if we drink and linger?
Does the Forbidden Garden
require the Emperor
to bless its blooming?

Girl, let us drink ourselves silly!
Just as my poem will come
to the beat of a little drum,
the buds and flowers, too,
leaning against the palace,
will listen and follow.

THE FLOATING THINGS

From Li Yu, Poem 8

The name of a thing
is not the thing.

A jade tree stands
at courtyard's front,
yet leaves that drop from it
are not hard stones
that can be carved
into dragons and lions.

They say the grass
is strewn with gems
when frost kisses it.
I reach for them
and my wet hand
is none the richer.

"To flower" means
making something new,
yet wilted peonies,
and stiff chrysanthemums
shame the garden,
like crones who came
to beg, and never left.

The moon, they say,
is full again.
Was it not full before?

Is this year's light
that shines from it
a newer thing, or just
the same old radiance,
shed from a tattered robe
in the night sky?

And if a thing's attributes
are not themselves
things in themselves,
moon just moon,
and flowers just flowers,
what thing is Youth
if pulled apart
from years and bodies?

Can Heaven grant us
this thing we most crave:
to age not
and to be young forever?

WOMAN OF SPRING

Adapted from Li Yu, Poem 9

Over the water
   the East Wind blows.
Over the hills
   the Sun holds on
a little longer.

Thanks to Spring,
I have more leisure time,
more hours for love
   and poetry.
Look: petals everywhere!
I leave them where they fall.

The drinking cups
   my artist friends abandoned,
tipped this way and that
by calligraphers and drummers,
flutists and lutenists,
some pink, some plum,
some celadon — mine
is the blue one, there —
their very scattering
around the old *Zun* vessel
empty now of wine:
this is a painting, too.
Somewhere a woman,
woman beyond empress,
lover or concubine,
visible to me only,
wakes from her long sleep.

She, too, is grateful
for the sun's long days.
The false peach face
she put on all winter
is faded now. No servant
comes to attend
    to her appearance
and correct her unruly
hair-knot. Heedless
even of what she is wearing,

this woman, nameless to me
and not of my retinue or court,
goes where she wishes. Her hand
seems to bless the bright land.
Upon a placid lake she views
her own face and blushes not.
Will she come back, alone,
at dusk, to tell me everything?

If I were painting this,
    I would place her *there*,
half-in, half-out of the pavilion,
arms and elbows
leaning across the balustrade.

Will she come as I bid her?
Will she take wine, or bring me some?
Will she at last, whisper
    her name into my ear?

MAKING LOVE
TO THE EMPRESS

After Li Yu, Poem 10

She was ready, but I could hardly wait.
I burst into her chamber, just as the last
of her preparations for love were underway.
I caught her fanning the censer
so that more sandalwood would blow
my way. She laughed, and that lilac-bud
of a little tongue circled her cherry lips
and moistened them. Before I could
turn to embrace her, one arm took up
the lute, and in her lap it went, a guard
against my haste. She tuned, oh, quickly!
to pretend to tune when she had tuned
before! and this to cool my ardor.
Forth the clean song issued —
ah, swan and peony, dove and cherry! —

I knelt to listen, and to aim
my upward-looking eyes into hers,
turned down to frets and fingering
(small darts of desire I thought I saw,
not just in melody,

but in the slight tremble she added
to every falling note.) A scent,
she must have meant to madden me,
rose and then faded from sleeves of gauze.
Why trick me with chemistry
when you have already conquered China?

And so we drank, and soon her cup
was tinged with wine, and fringed
with the hue of abducted cherry.
At last, the *pi-pa*[1] put aside, the song
having reached its triple ending,
she lay there stretched, all limbs in view
upon the silk embroidered bed.
Oh, what is modesty, when thunder strikes
and blinds the eyes, unbearable!

When my sight cleared, and what I saw
I saw again, she parted her lips, and
from her mouth a cascade of red petals,
blew up and out. I nearly fainted.

---

[1] *Pi-pa.* The Chinese lute.

SWEEPING THE TOMBS

After Li Yu, Poem 11

So many trees above,
almost no sky. Lazy,
I linger alone in the hut
the caretaker lives in.
Ancient pines moan,
whisper my father's name,
and his, and his.

This early April night
might go on forever. Warm now,
a moment later I am shivering.
Cold nights will soon be over.

The Feast of Qingming
ended just yesterday.
With my own hands I swept
the tomb of my father,
and his, and his.

Others swept clean of leaves
and sand and pebbles,
the graves of imperial uncles,
of consorts whose names
nobody remembers,
and of several dread dowagers
whose ghosts demanded
    extra incense
and more circling 'round
as the prayers went up.

Ancestors appeased,
the earth is free
to mark the end of Spring.

The out-of-focus moon
is its own ghost tonight.
Clouds roll, and down the slope
a breeze torments
the budding peach and apricot.

Who is impatient for summer?
And who, down there,
sits on a swing and chatters,
laughing and gossiping?

My heart is one with myself,
but for my land and its people,
ten thousand threads of thought
go out to who knows where
for who knows what response.

Even the Son of Heaven
cannot find room enough
to untangle one small web
of one night's thoughts.

Given the whole world
to unravel it, I still would not
have any idea
what I am supposed to do.

Those below earth
and in the sky, lend me
at least, if nothing else,
a calm demeanor.

DOWN SOUTH

From Li Yu, Poem 12

Down South, they know what to do
    with springtime.
There, when my thoughts turn away
from duty and empire, I imagine myself,
where the spring is already well in progress.

Now every lake floats the pleasure boats,
the *er-hu*[1] fiddles hum like bees, flute girls
exchange shy looks with the young scholars.
The green-faced rivers are drunk
    with willows,
towns dust-clogged with trees' yellow catkins.
More flowers bloom than eye or hand can capture.

Busy are those who watch this blossoming,
trying in vain with brush to draw it,
so quickly is it here and gone.
Busier still are their sleepless nights
when one beside another they lay
entwined, and the high stars call them.

---

[1] *Er-hu*. The Chinese violin, a fiddle with two strings.

THE FORBIDDEN PALACE

From Li Yu, Poem 13

Some silly concubines believe
the Palace is the Universe.
Yet once, each arrived here
knowing nothing. At first,
they sent packages back home
to sisters, grandmothers.
Then they forgot,
    as every new day
        became a forever.

I hear them chattering
of how some distant hill
marks the Palace boundary.
Then on a clearer day
another hill behind it
presents itself, and *that*
is the world's far edge.

In truth, I cannot walk
or ride from one end to another
in a single day. It just goes on,
as ancestors appended hill
and valley, stream and forest.

Paintings are made
showing its lakes, gardens,
pavilions and vistas.
No scroll is wide enough, or high,
to do my palace grounds justice.
This truly is the heart of the world.

Yes, armies go forth;
    some come back shattered.
Yes, taxes and tributes come,
    and strangers kow-tow and beg.
In places I have never heard of,
they say the word "China" and sigh.

Strange it is
that the heart of China sighs,
and knows not for whom or why.
I cannot touch the hills.
The sky's clouds defy my reach.
The water today
is unclear and cold:
the tea will not be right.

All summer I have been distracted.
I am thinking of the one
I am no longer allowed to see.
The leaves were still green
when she was taken from me,
and soon they will blaze red.

By trick and subterfuge,
an order forged, my seal affixed,
she has been carted off by night.
The Empress does not will her death,
but keeps her far away somewhere.
I dare not speak, I dare not ask.
It is as though she had never existed.

The opening chrysanthemum,
as it drinks in the sun,
mocks me. It closes, satisfied.
Swans at the edge of vision
fly, each with his mate up high.
No one gives them orders.

I am alone. I call for no one.
The concubines had might as well
be cemetery crows for all
I care about their caresses now.

The moon tugs earth and tides.
The mocking breeze pulls
at my curtains randomly.
Brush to paper,
I do not have the will to write.

I wait for something
    to mean something.

VISITING THE DOWAGER

Adapted from Li Yu, Poem 14

What does this old woman know
    that I do not?
I am Emperor of Everything
    but cannot translate why

her hair, already streaked with gray,
falls to her shoulder in disarray,
or why the furrow between
her eyebrows is deeper yet
than what it was before.

What cause has she
to be unhappy?
She has her own servant,
an out-of-the-way
pavilion, well-situated.
She wants no company.
Many are unaware
she is still alive.
I pay my respects
at suitable intervals.

Putting aside the gifts
I brought for her —
green tea, a scroll
with my new poems,
and a fine crackle-glaze
vase with dragons —

I aim a gaze, quizzical
and open my hands,
imploring her. Instead
of addressing me,

she leans one cheek upon
one opened hand, pale
as a bamboo shoot,
and then inclines her head,
eyes shut,
toward the residence.

Word came to her just now,
as she leaned over the balcony.
Servants below have passed
it all to one another in a string
of echoes. Through tears she says:

"Son of my son,
go to the Empress —
your child has died."

THE OTHER WOMAN

From Li Yu, Poem 15

The cherry petals came too late;
they carpet the steps,
but the Empress does not notice them.

I sit by the bed and tend
    the covered brazier;
its fire is almost gone
    and the tea already made
is lukewarm now.
No matter, for she has taken none.

A year has passed since grief arrived.
Each day without
the young prince's laughter
is as sad as the one before.

Being beautiful for me,
or for her own pleasure,
seems a thing of the past.
Her face looks wrong,
the double-knotted hair
off-kilter; her eyes
are almost blank,

like the thin clouds
that mark a gloomy day.
Dried tears spot-stain
her vermilion vest.

My back is turned.
Why do I yearn so bitterly
for the younger face
that is the same face?
Why do I think of *her*
as I day-dream
at the window lattice?

THE EMPRESS, ALONE

Adapted from Li Yu, Poem 16

She has given up waiting.
In lamplight, her face
will not even fill a mirror:
a sliver of brow and cheek
glow pale, like the new moon's
sickly crescent.
                    To do her hair,
with that elaborate coif
of cicada and phoenix,
that once so pleased him,
the jade pin, and the silver
one, lay ready on her table.
She picks them up.
She puts them down.

What is the use?
He is watching somewhere,
or someone is watching
on his behalf.
"Tell me: Is the Empress unhappy?"
"Tell me: Does she bother
to make herself presentable?"

The lazier she grows,
the more disheveled she is,
the less he is likely
to come to her.

Can she give him
another heir?
Does she want to?
No one even asks.

The double curtains
that brought him unannounced
so many evenings
into her chamber,
are as still as stone.
Her eyes dart up and out
to the palace and its terraces.
No lights. All are asleep.
He did not choose her.
He did not choose anyone.
He will not come.

As the flower fades,
as the fickle wind
goes where it wills,
all must change without her.

When a wheel turns,
the axle is compelled to follow,
as it draws up water
from the golden well.

Will she drink,
or will she leave the cup
unemptied?

It is better to have wine,
and to wake up forgetful.
Will the morning sun care
that she begged for Spring?
Worrying is worse
than any sickness.

THE PRISONER

After Li Yu, Poem 17

I have found her! As in a sad tale,
an evil fairy prevailed.
The world's most beautiful woman
is confined to a room so narrow
two arms can almost touch
the heavy and well-planked walls.

A tiny terrace extends from it,
and there I saw her at last,
leaning at risk of a fall
over the balustrade, too high,
bare rocks below a certain death
to anyone foolish enough to jump.
All this, and on the palace grounds!

I found the door, concealed
within a grotto, and there she stood!

Food there was, and a tiny brazier,
all the best and the finest tea.
She had fine garments here,
all the jewels one could wish for,
even a small bronze Bodhisattva:

Not a cell, like one
a Buddhist nun
or monk might occupy,
but a doll-house
pavilion for one!

Her rival did not intend it so,
but it was a temple to our passion.
O narrow bed! All pillows thrown aside,
she drew me quietly there. We stood,
we knelt, we melted like ingots
in the fire that purifies. I held the key
to the room in my hands. She took it.
We laughed, and planned our future.
We looked at one another, and now I knew
what a conspiracy was, and what its vows.

But as for here and now,
the bed just wide enough for one,
is also wide enough for two.

WAITING FOR HER

After Li Yu, Poem 18

The rain falls so hard, I squint
and cannot uncurl my eyebrows.
The red petals, undone, are washed
away in streams and rivulets
until I cannot see them.
Spring floods are underway.

Streams will be high,
some paths, impassable.
Even when rain is done,
I hear nothing.
The copied key inside
undoes the one her captors
made to hide her. Free,
she can move like a ghost
on any moonless night.

No sign of her. Incense has burned
down to the nub and seal. The light
of my night-candle is nearly gone.
How much longer? What agony
that if I go to sleep, she comes
to me anyway, but cold, serene,
as thin as a cloud, untouchable.

THE HUT

After Li Yu, Poem 19

Like bandits we meet
at an abandoned hut.
We pretend to be peasants,
engaged in some illicit
love affair. This is our game.
She plays the bamboo flute, not well,
but I delight at her fingers at play
as she creates a new melody.

The glances she steals, the way
she looks at me, as though
I were a new bridegroom,
enchant me. I feel as high
as the sea-waves in autumn,
as full as a rain-cloud ready
to burst. Our love-cries rise,
embroidering the night sky
with comets and falling stars.

They are saying I am no Emperor,
that our dynasty has been demoted
to a mere kingdom, that I must send
my brother as prince, a hostage
almost certainly, to this Song king
who calls himself an emperor.

They say I only care
about love and music and poetry.

Guilty! After such ecstasy, all
is as nothing to me. Or all is one
within me. The whole wide world
is a day-dream in springtime.

THE BELOVED SPEAKS

After Li Yu, Poem 20

The flowers were bright
   (and might have lit my way like lanterns)
but the moon was diffused in light mist.
Cool, but not too cold,
that was the best night to go to my lover.
Trembling I trod the perfumed stones,
step upon step amid the night-blooms.
I held in one hand the golden-threaded shoes,
in the other his scroll of urgent summoning.

South of the newly-painted hall,
in the appointed place I met him.
His face was turned away and upward
as though he searched the moon's face
or with his hawk-fierce eye some dove
asleep on a still and leafy branchlet.

At first, I leaned against him, shivering;
my pale arms could not encompass
the sweep of his cloaked broad shoulders.
He made a sound that might have been
my name, or merely sighed, exhaling.
I said, "I cannot come as often now,
so tonight you must love me twice as hard."

THE INTERRUPTION

After Li Yu, Poem 21

He had made
a new dress for her,
and things to match:
light-colored green her gown
silk thin as gauze,
head-band a string of clouds
of gleaming mother-of-pearl,
the necklace of jade beads
which she bites playfully
instead of letting them drop
to grace her girlish
figure. Why does she frown?

He has done everything for her
that a secret lover can. More
is impossible. Old wives frown,
and ministers find texts
that would condemn them.

And what is better, after all,
than the love that is not
allowed? Autumn has come;
with longer nights, they could
stay together longer.
Why does she hesitate?
She has not even thanked him.
What woman else
would be so dressed
and undressed by her lover?

This is a new spot, not far
from the Imperial gardens.
It is more dangerous for them,
and all the more delicious.
A tall tree, uncommon,
drops yellow fruit unknown
beyond the tropics.[1]
One could hear them fall.
Peeled, they yield
erotic fragrances.

Just as the Emperor reaches
to embrace his slave and idol,
the door bursts open, a man
in shadow lunges in,
then kneels. Li Yu
recognizes Counselor Lin.

"Rise!" he says. "How dare you
interrupt me here?"

"Your M-Majesty!" the man stutters.
He does not look at the woman.

"Who knows that I am here?"—
"Those sworn to protect you
always know where you are.
Would you not wish it so?" —

"I wish to have *secrets*,"
the Emperor shouts.
"Are you not a man yourself?" —

---

[1] *Yellow fruit unknown* ... A banana tree.

"The Empress knows all,"
Lin ventures to tell him.
"She has known for a week!"

At this, a small shriek
issues from the cringing girl.
She removes the head-band,
the string of jade.

"Majesty, I have known you
since the day of your birth.
And so it is that I am asked
to be the one to tell you …"

"To tell me, what?"

"That Empress Zhou,
your queen and ours,
was found dead one hour ago."

ALONE IN THE TEMPLE

Li Yu, after the death of Empress Zhou

Lord Buddha, why?

Silence.
Incense rising,
a vertical line
no breeze disturbs.
It is as though the world
stopped breathing.

That there is no answer,
is an answer.

Lord Buddha, why?
Look everywhere
inside our realm.
Are not the finest
peaks surmounted
by your temples?
Have we not carved
you into cliffs, filled
grottoes with shrines?

Do we not have as many
monks as scholars?
As many Bodhisattva
figures as soldiers?
As many stupas
as bell and drum towers?
As many prayer wheels
as chariots?

Those who would topple the last
of Tang — they do not know you.
We fight, but of all deaths
this one death I cannot
accept with calm resolve.

She is gone! Her shroud
is even now rolled up
and carried to the chamber.
I must watch as her ashes
rise to the heavens.

Have you not taught
there is no peace
until there is no will
to war? I have no will
to war. Love was my
barricade. It fell.

The people, in loving me,
loved you. What now,
Lord Buddha, what?

Who the illusion,
you, or I?

THE COURT OFFICIALS

"Son of Heaven!"
 "Your Majesty!"
  "Great King!"
they shouted, knelt,
and timidly approached.

The Court was dark.
Weeks of mourning,
chaos, actually.
Moths fluttered
around the silk tapestries,
the throne, untenanted,
gathered dust.

"You are here about the Rituals,"
he answered from shadow.
They could not see his face.
"Do as was always done.
Consult the oracles, lay out
the calendars of mourning.

"I would as soon hear bells
and laughter again,
street-vendor songs outside
the walls, the drums and gongs
of the theater. When mourning
ends for all, it need not end for me."

"Son of Heaven, all will be done
as in your father's and grandfather's
time, and as all China has done
since the First Emperor's era."

He nods. He waves a hand
to dismiss them.

They do not remove themselves.

"Your Majesty!" one calls again.

"Is there more?"
                "We beg to ask
what you mean to do
about — about the *woman*."

"Who knows of this?" he asks,
in a tone of ice and danger.

"Every bird repeats it. Each branch
of the willow tree sings about it."

"Well, then," he sighs. "I mean
to make her Empress. Call her
Empress Zhou the Younger."

One courtier groans, another
beats his head against the plank
he carried to make appeal.
"Oh, call her a concubine!"
one begs. "A consort, a consort!"
the other two implore.

"With her dead sister, my Empress,
she has equal rank. Why now,
should I not honor and elevate
one who is devoted to me alone?"

"Because of the gossips,
O Son of Heaven. You do not know
what calumnies they invent,
lies you invite by circumstance." —

"Explain." —

"They will make her out worse
than Empress Wu. Tales they invent
will say she murdered the young prince,
hating a nephew born to the throne.
They will say she lured you with magic,
used drugs and sorcery to seduce,
so that you could not tell
one woman from another.
They will say she procured poisons,
and one will come forth and say
she bought them of his neighbor
who sells those drugs and charms
that cancel wives and children." —

"She is above reproach." —
"A thousand lies will follow her
like clouds of angry gnats,
and a thousand times repeated
they will be truths to many.
Spare her and you, we beg you.
Do not elevate this woman."

After a long pause, in which
the three officials trembled,
he stiffly ordered:

"These three things I command.
Publish the Calendar of Rituals.
Announce the elevation
    of Empress Zhou the Younger.
These things done, collect
   your pensions.

"The gossips you warn me about
    are you."

DOUBTS

Adapted from Li Yu, Poem 22

As everything fades,
    the cherry flowers
    are not what they were;
limp, they fall,
    fallen, they rot.

Spring is not
    what it used to be
when you loved me
    better.

They have clouded my mind
    with idle gossip;
yours, with doubt and regret.
Harming no one,
    we now harm all.

I passed beneath the gate
onto the covered porch.
The night had ended.
From here I watched
the moon slant down
upon the withered branches.

The hut was still.
No pale lamp fluttered.
I waited for you
until the dawning light
made it impossible to stay.

That night I waited,
watched, and did not enter,
you had arrived before me
and fell into
a contented sleep.

I went my way,
    turned back,
and saw you going
    the other.

I think of it now.
I never told you.

THE FUTILE BOUQUET

After Li Yu, Poem 23

There is a forest flower
I love, found only
one week of the Spring
in just one shady wooded spot.

I go with poets there,
and painters, and each of us
attempt to catch
    that flower's essence.

Today my servants
have brought me some:
ripped from their soil,
poor droopy things
they are, the red
already gone to orange,
the petals withering,
stalks oozing milky white.

Kidnapped flowers,
what ransom can I give,
what favor confer
on the violated forest?

A wine I know
has the same vermilion hue.
Tears of the grape? My tears
that ought to be my blood?

Send wine! Call in
some poets to console me.
Find some drear song
to fiddle me to sleep.
Life is now a misery.
Onward it carries me
eastward against my will
with the relentless floods.

LONG IS THE SADNESS

After Li Yu, Poem 24

Weep, China!
    The girl who played the flute
    among the trees, and charmed
    an Emperor, is gone.
The Spring light comes seeking her
    in the royal garden,
clouds of sweet pollen, and petals
    of gold, cascade in waves,
seeking her out, and finding
    only a funeral.
Winds from the East
    that lifted me once
    now make me stoop,
unbearable now the fragrance
    it carries.

I watch the moon pass
the cut and curve of the jade window;
    waning, diminished, sliced.

Will I come to see the days
    of my misery outnumbering
the days I was allotted joy?
(Who should live so long?)

Beyond the balcony a willow
    droops with its own weight
    of leaf and branch to water,
expecting to find a companion —
hopes dashed, it only sees
    itself reflected. No wonder
we say the splendid tree weeps.

Dressed in mourning,
    one scarcely has time for love.
Each time I meet
    the one who waits for me,
it is as short as a dream.
      Haste wounds us.

We part. I am sure
there are certain words she hopes for
that I am not prepared to say,
not with so fresh a ghost
listening.

NIGHTMARE

How many faces greet you
when your grateful eyes open,
remembering the night of love?

Just one? Or, one,
and the one who resembled her,
and is now ashes?

How many feet
peep out beneath the blankets?
Pray to the gods it is not six!

PRISONER OF THE SONG EMPEROR

MEDITATION IN EXILE

Adapted from Li Yu, Poem 25

I know I should go in, now.
It is best to forget it all, better to sleep
and recall it to ghost-life; least-best
is waiting out the night here,
thinking of those who have gone.

The wind is back in the courtyard —
new wind or ever the same one? —
and the dull grass is sliced
    with new green slivers.

Spring, undeniable, paints yellow-green
    in willow shoots.
Long I recline on the balustrade,
waving away my servant, a nay
to the tonic of the waiting teacup.

I am alone. I am not
among the endless scrolls of my old poems —
gone and lost! I mouth the words
of those I can remember — others
must be my memorial called forth
to the minds of surviving friends.
My mouth seems full of stones,
my words, choked back.

                All ears,
I wait for the next west-east
fluttering amid the bamboo leaves,
in wind a new moon always prompts.

Away, where I am missed
and amid those I despair of,
exactly the same sky shivers.

Rubbing their hands
    together, the *pi-pa* players
await my orders. What tune
can I order amid the willow rush,
the ruffle of wind in the cat-tails?
I gesture them to stillness. They bow.
They think me unmusical.
The melodies they want to play
are not the ones I know.

Someone, I see, has not removed
the hundred-year-old wine jar,
nor my ink pot and its brushes.
As for calligraphy, what is mine
against that cracked-ice poem
that just now melts on the lake?
Once, I would have indicated that
with but one finger, and someone
would have rushed to draw it.

On the deep, dark terrace behind me
a single candle burns, one ember
beside it, incense out of breath.

The past. The past. The dawn
that I am facing is solitary;
there seems scant need to undress
but to rise and re-dress again,
for whom, or for what?

One palace is like
another palace; the same earth
turns below home and exile.
Here, there is the pretense
    of status and honor.
Who am I to complain?
I could well write
another thousand poems.

I feel in my hair the gnawing frost,
as on my brow the last snow
hovers at edge of vision
and refuses to melt.

I   will   just   sit.

But how can words come
when thought is unthinkable?

NIGHT SOUNDS

After Li Yu, Poem 26

I think they mean to torture me
with either silence, or sounds.
When my residence is empty
as I have no visitors at all,
the quiet of the courtyard
seems weirdly ominous.
It makes me hear
sounds no one wants,
such as the pounding
of laundry on cold stones.
Sometimes it is the wind,
which howls in this country
with unpleasant vowels.

Why are the nights so long?
Sleep is insufficient
to cover them.
Ears are worse than eyes
in a strange place.

Among the pines,
and worse, among
the rattling bamboo,
what creatures here
prowl nocturnally?

Sounds in the night
that enter my curtained
windows — how many
belong to those
who watch and count
my every movement?

If I sound out a poem,
subversive and sad,
to whose ears
will they repeat it?

MONOTONY

After Li Yu, Poem 27

Wood against wood,
stalk against stalk,
pounding like gongs
all day, all night.

I swear, that even
when wind diminishes,
the rattling goes on.

Beneath a moon
heartless as a block of ice,
I don a coat to walk
around the courtyard.

I scan the bamboo grove
for mischief. Miscreants
are out there; no poems
come amid the clack-clack,
rick-rack of the stalks,
the flutter-flap of leaves
like birds tethered
and trying to escape.

No one is there.
No tormentors sit
with block and clapper
charged with disturbing me.

Here, Nature abhors me.
Life may be long,
but bamboo is longer.

NINTH DAY
OF THE NINTH MONTH

After Li Yu, Poem 28

In autumn, the daylight hastens away.
Red leaves pile up and clog the stairs.
The ninth day of the ninth month
has come and gone — the Double Yang
Festival. Brooms sweep the houses.
Hills groan with pilgrims' footsteps.
Joss-merchants sell money to burn.
Chrysanthemums are crushed to make
a heady liqueur for this time only.

By now, the climbing dog rose
sheds its frail petals back at home,
painting with pink my old pavilions.
While here, the still-abundant flowers,
purple and full, perfume the garden.

I am told I have no right to complain.
Smoke from the kitchens huddles low
as thin rain damps it down. Here every
dog and exile eats his fill each day.

The first arriving swans are gathering.
In pairs, they sing sad songs in unison.
They came, I am reminded, free-willed.
I sigh, and swallow hard. Thus
it will be for me, as the gray sky drops
an exile's bitter sorrow.

THE PARASOL TREES

After Li Yu, Poem 29

People whose names I did not
even know — how I miss them!
Seldom did I ask of one
who served me: what province,
what town, what branch
of what respected family?

Alone, with no one
whose opinion I value
to ask for, no one
to command some small
and trivial favor from,
I am wordless. This one,
who keeps a safe distance
and bows, has large ears.
He is here to spy.
That one, who goes and fetches
for me, is greedy for bribes.
A grunt is their salute.
They joke with one another
in a dialect unknown to me.

I go to the grove's west end;
my shadow follows. It is here,
in one break of the tree-line
I might stand and paint
the way the waxing moon hangs
a pendant hook. A star
it brushes in front of, shimmers —
perhaps it is a planet, a fellow
wanderer far from his own home.

Behind me, a formal courtyard
lined with parasol trees
hems autumn in, a prisoner.
Each *wutong* tree
    awaits its phoenix;
none come, and green
has faded to yellow.
Each leaf is wide enough
    to hold a poem,
each, in breaking away,
is a sign of parting.

Of this, I need no reminder.
I say "Return!" It says, "No more."
Hands full of these damp
and wingless birds, I try
to untangle them. Vein, stem,
and branchlet cling, clog,
and fall. Cold wind and frost
will sort them out. Dispersed,
they fall impaled on other trees.

Not one will ever see its brother
again. The trees themselves
will hoard small clumps, in niche
of bark and bole, like a mother's
sickly and favorite children.

No use, sad colonnade
of parasol trees. No use!
We are held to the ground
by gravity, by paving stones
that hold us, root and heart.

The court spy regards me:
a madman, muttering
words incomprehensible,
stuffing his robes
with rotting, pungent leaves.
Li Yu, the lunatic!

SEPARATED

After Li Yu, Poem 30

No one will say
why I am not allowed
to see you. Spring broke
the day our hands last touched,
and now the Spring
is half the way to Summer.

Everything I loved
in your presence
annoys me now.
Plum blossoms fall
and pile in drifts,
blow in my face
as I brush them aside.
They are no longer
beautiful to me.

A stupid swan has come
and perched itself
on my window-sill.
What does she mean
to tell me? What language
does a swan speak,
anyway? And where has it been?

Can it carry a dream to me
of you and of our time together?

Here we came, a pair of exiles,
and now, from one another
exiled again, and to what end?

Remember the games we played,
the contests among the poets?
Now, if one came up and asked me,
"What is the sorrow of parting like?"

I know how to answer:

It is the one thing
both eternal and infinite.
The sorrow of parting
is like new grass in spring;
the farther you look,
the more there seems to be.

THE LAND OF WINE

After Li Yu, Poem 31

Wind and rain,
   more wind,
      more rain.
The curtain goes
   horizontal,
the screen
   with its dismal painting
     wobbles this way and that
     and almost tumbles.

The lamp falters.
The water-clock must be about
its business, but I hear no drips
in all this autumnal uproar.

Turning my head left,
   turning my head right,
there is no comfort:
what devil fashioned
these pillows, anyway?
Sitting or lying down,
sleep is impossible,
rest an illusion.

I shall be useless tomorrow.

Perhaps being useless
is an exile's business.
The affairs of the world
do not require me.

I can make much ado
about dressing myself,
walk to the court
with secret agent in tow
and pretend to have
   something to say
      to one who calls himself
      my better.

And while I wait,
   in one of a dozen
   anterooms, someone
will bow and offer wine,
   a better one
than what I have here,
and after one or two cups
I shall slip away,
   forgetful of what
   my business was.

They will mock me,
but if my destiny is just
to float about haphazardly,
let me at least
be drunk on a decent
   vintage.

TEARS

After Li Yu, Poem 32

So many tears! Like rivers
on the map of China,
sideways they flow
across my furrowed cheeks.

Tears cannot tell my story;
    ink can.
Tears cannot play the phoenix
    flute; breath can.

I weep, I write, I sigh.
Still this failing heart
    refuses to break.

HORSES AS FIERCE
AS FLYING DRAGONS

After Li Yu, Poem 33

Dreams hurt.
Last night I thought
I was back in my palace.
My feet knew every turn
and by-way. Nothing
was changed. Bronzes
and vases and carvings,
all were intact. Fresh
flowers adorned everything.

War drums were sounding.
Chariots flared out
    in every direction,
horses as fierce
    as flying dragons.

The breeze behaved.
The upright flowers
stood at full attention.

Who would have called
the world that we knew,
too good to be true?

LICHEN

After Li Yu, Poem 34

Save sorrow for what is gone forever,
a wise one advises me. Creature
of habit that I am, everything
here depresses me. The sight
of Nature ought to soothe and heal,
but Grief is my looking-glass.

The humble lichen,
    so fond of rocks
    and branches,
ascends the neglected
    stairs as well.
I do not disturb
    its melancholy advance.

The curtain, edged
    with pearls, sways
    lazily, thin barricade
against the autumn breeze.

No one strides in
    with orders or requests,
pushing aside the cloth,
nor do soft steps
    of timid feet pause
and await my summoning.
    I had a Golden Saber once;
like me and my pride,
it is someone's trophy now.

I had a mansion of jade,
a palace of dark
    chalcedony,
pavilions too numerous
    to catalog.
Looted and desolate,
they cast long shadows
upon the Qinhuai River.

Above the headless flowers
    killed by frost,
the moon blazons
    in the transparent sky.

AM I AWAKE?

After Li Yu, Poem 35

Endless rain falls
    in waves and ripples.
Spring is finally retiring.

Yet I shiver beneath
    the silken coverlet,
wary of braving cold air
    before the sun's warming.

Am I awake? Exile
    no longer,
I long for old pleasures.
As sudden as it was morn,
it is evening. I lean
against the parapet,
my mountains, *my* rivers
clear in view.

All too easy
    was the departure in haste,
    not a moment to spare
    in backward-looking —
yet how I ached to see the sights
    coming, one by one,
as the old places returned to view.

Beyond the hill, the flood waters
gather up all the refugee
petals, rushing them away
as Spring invades and conquers.

Where does Spring die, I wonder —
on Earth, or in the Heavens?

Then up I sit, and rub my eyes.
This is no house of mine.
No scrolls, no paintings, no wall
filled top to bottom with poetry!
Again and forever, those dreams of home!

PLACES AND NAMES

After Li Yu, Poem 36

Best are the names
the places themselves tell you.
Like candles that gutter
    up and out,
or weeds borne randomly
    on errant waves,
one dream recurs.

I see the land my fathers won,
but in it are men unfamiliar,
costumes and accents wrong.
I try to introduce myself,
but I am waved away
    as a madman.
Heaven has set me adrift,
not to be known,
            but still to know
the reason for each place's
naming. This little wood —
can it be anything except
the "Bower Awaiting Moon?"

This westward-facing spot
is nothing if it is not
"The Shading-Flower Terrace."

Will all of Tang be truly gone
when all the names are lost?

OF TRYSTS GONE BY

After Li Yu, Poem 37

Now that I know too much
I am almost embarrassed
to watch the Spring unfold.

Flowers doing what flowers do
remind me of trysts gone by,
of acting without rhyme or reason.

The trusty willow trees shelter me.
My confidants, they have seen it all,
and they do not trouble themselves
with random love affairs.

Their green-and-gray shagginess
brushes against my weary head.
In their cool indifferent shade
I could sleep all day.

EMPTY IS THE PAST

After Li Yu, Poem 38

Does some persistent bumblebee
come to my fluttering eyes
expecting dream-nectar?

How disappointed
   he must be!
I am a sour well,
   a soap-work,
   an iron forge,
   a leather tannery.

I have no good word,
   or thought, or prayer,
   for anyone.

Sorrow I cannot escape,
   except in the dreams
that make me even more
   miserable.

What wakes me up?
What forces me
   to greet another day?
There is a thread
   that pulls my eyelids open,
made from dried tears
   that stick to my face
from cheek to beard.

Oh, to stand atop
   an autumn terrace
with someone, anyone,
   beside me!

WHAT KIND OF POET?

After Li Yu, Poem 39

What kind of poet am I
   who cannot bear spring flowers
   or the flush of autumn?

What kind of poet am I
   who shuns the moon's
      beckoning,
when all I can do
   is to ask it,
"Do you see my lost kingdom?"

What kind of poet am I
   who no longer retells
     the exploits of his father,
     the daring of ancestors,
     the courage of mothers?
Having no seal, I shall
   soon enough be nameless.

What kind of poet am I
   who can no longer adorn
   a painting with calligraphy,
   or compel a painter
   to illustrate his words?

Who cares what I think,
   or what I have suffered?

No one.

Without me, the carved
jade balcony and winding stairs
may still be there, but those
who walked them
   will be less than ghosts
if no one writes of them.

Do some back home
   still read my lines
and ask of one another
the measure of Li Yu's pain?

How many pieces can one
be sliced into?

How many drops flow
into the Qinhuai River,
and the Yellow River too?

Those numbers ought to be
just about right.

WRITTEN WHILE DYING

For Emperor Li Yu (937 – 978 CE)

Now I am dead.
There is no other way
to write this poem
except backwards.

Because Taizong
resented my last poems
(who would not yearn
for what he has lost?) —
because I am said to be
all things considered,
a better poet.

Because I cared less
with each day's passing,
wife torn from me,
a weeping shell of herself,
since she was raped
by the Song Emperor.

Because I will not address
that personage correctly,
because I am now called,
not "former Emperor," not King,
not as Li Congjia, the name
my father gave me,
the name to which
all people and foreigners
knelt and kow-towed,
but by an epithet:
Marquis of Wei Wing
(Lord of Edicts Disobeyed).

Now I am dead,
because my generals came
with warlike strategy,
and I dismissed them,
preferring my evenings
in the Poets' Pavilion,
with painters and artists
who fled to me from
every other kingdom.

Now I am dead,
because my captive brother
summoned, implored,
my travel to Song's capital,
and I went not. Instead
I sent poems and art,
the best ambassadors
of peace and accord.

Now I am dead.
No armor did I don,
no chariot ascend
when the invaders came.

I was in the temple,
composing a poem,
surrounded by monks,
incense, and prayer wheels,
when they broke in
and seized me. Where
was the magic, then?

Now I am dead,
because wise counselors
wanted me strict, cruel,
and cunning, like those
who raced to crush
our borders. Refusing,

I sent them home.
Some killed themselves
in honor's name.
It was I who killed them!

Now I am dead,
who tried to have
one woman as wife,
and her younger sister, too.
As for the two women,
one died, and then I married
the other. Is that not honorable?
Did I not carve,
with my own hand
two thousand characters
on the Empress's tombstone?

Those who forbade my love,
and my second marriage,
I sent home to their villages
to live until their beards
touched ground.
Now their ghosts haunt me.

Now I am dead,
because I drank a cup,
an overflowing cup
of heart-warm wine,
best of the southern
vineyards, I was told.

Because my dishonored wife
put her pale hand
upon the celadon vessel
to taste it first,
and a soldier pushed
her aside and said,

>   "This wine is for one,
from the Emperor's table.
The Marquis only must drink."

"I am not thirsty," I said.

"The Marquis must drink.
I must say at his table
that you have tasted it,
and in full proof of pleasure,
have drained it to the dregs."
Now I am dead,
because the willows of home
have wept two years for me;
twice have I left unswept
the tombs of my fathers;
twice have I failed to lift
up in the dead's honor
a flagon of chrysanthemum;
and twice has the Lunar Year
come and gone in a place
that no longer has my name.

Peace be to you, Song Emperor,
and to all peoples. I am still
King of leaves and petals, Lord
of moonlight and sudden breezes.
Who will they read
a thousand years from now?

Now I —

ABOUT THE POEMS

This volume collects all of my poems to date that are based upon, or inspired by Chinese people, literature, art, and history.

My first encounter with Chinese culture was a brief but memorable act of hospitality. When I arrived at Edinboro State College in 1969, virtually an orphan and as penniless as any student has even been, I was employed at the college library. The head librarian there was Dr. Hwa-Wei Lee, a Fujian-born librarian, scholar, and translator. In August of that first summer, I was invited to tea and for a meal celebrating the Chinese Moon Festival. There I had my first good tea, served by Mrs. Lee, and sampled several moon cakes, which I was told came "all the way from Toronto." From such small, civilized gestures are planted the seeds of curiosity.

When I lived in San Francisco in 1967, I was thrust into a city with a rich Chinatown, but the barriers between the two cultures were impermeable. I was engaged in my Haight-Ashbury Hippie culture exploration, and San Francisco's Chinatown was not part of this world.

Everything changed several years later in New York City, when I gained the friendship of a cultured, young, spoiled new arrival from Taiwan. Then did I gain entry, and patient introduction, to Chinese art, music, literature, film, and cuisine. A culture that everyone around me scorned and ridiculed, was finally unfolding its grandeur and glory before me.

The story of my friendship is told frankly in the poem, "The Loft on Fourteenth Street." Since then I have continued my Chinese explorations, through reading, lectures, films, auction-house previews of Chinese art sales, and attending live Chinese operas in New York and Boston. It has been, for the most part, a solitary passion, and I feel a great kinship with the idealized life shown in Chinese art: the scholar taking tea in his gazebo amid pine trees, surrounded by antiques brought out to sun and air, and in companionship of poets and musicians. But I am also keenly aware that the real life of people in the real China is a continuation of the travail its people have endured for millennia. One tyranny replaces another, and the intervals of peace are sweet but brief. Even if the Twilight Zone China of scholarly imagination is an intellectual invention, it is not a Western exploitation or appropriation, for the Chinese themselves indulge in this idealization of an aloof life spent in the contemplation of nature. The British have their own equivalents in pastoral poetry and Arthurian Camelot. The grass is always greener on the other side of the fence of time.

"Chinatown, 1975" is a recollection of sitting at dinner with a group of young Chinese men, who explained to me some of the class distinctions made among the people in New York's Chinatown.

The recent poem, "The Thirteen Scorpions" is a work of my time as much as a snapshot of a long-lived and self-assured emperor. Giving a Jesuit missionary his due only serves to show off the narcissism of an Emperor who styles himself "the most interesting man who ever lived." Anyone alive in 2022 knows all too well what this is about. The "poetic monologue," a genre inherited from Robert Browning, provides the challenge of a single narrating voice with the viewer/listener implied, and such writings make good actors' pieces.

"The White Tiger" had a worldly impulse. I had befriended a Chinese graduate student at Brown University, whom I had given the nick-name of "Tiger," and when, just a day after I helped him work on his résumé, I approached him at a symphony concert and he pretended not to know me, I wrote a short poem of pique that culminated with the wise servant cautioning the scholar that the fickle tiger was not to be trusted.

Sometime later I returned to the poem, and the original version was completely superseded by the new triumphant and defiant ending. So delighted was I with what this poem became, that I made it the culminating poem of the second half of my autumn poem cycle, *Anniversarius: The Book of Autumn*.

"The Orphaned Vase" is simply my exploration of the possible history of a sad little Chinese vase, one of the first I acquired for my collection.

"Mrs. Wang's Rebellion" was part of a longer poem, "Arabesques on the Statue of Liberty," based on my sighting of a Chinese lady carrying a miniature Statue of Liberty down Canal Street. Her determined look convinced me that she was about some serious business.

"Figures on a Kangxi Vase" describes and interprets an "Ancients Drinking" blue-and-white vase I acquired in early 2023. While writing the poem I felt that the same poem might be composed in French, so I have added my rough-draft French version.

"The Azaleas of Ningpo" reflects the mixed admiration the Chinese have for azaleas and rhododendrons, to be admired from afar but not to be brought into the home.

"October Storm" was written in Weehawken, NJ. In 1998, after I had returned from San Francisco with a stone seal containing my chosen Chinese name (Meng Qiu Lei).

"The Emperor Kangxi Drinks Tea From Eggshell Porcelain Teacups" is a poem-cycle of 13 lyric poems, all written in one afternoon in February 2023. Only one day earlier, I had learned about fabulously rare sets of Ming-style wine cups made during the later reign of Qing Emperor Kangxi (1654-1722). The Emperor delighted in this collection of twelve hand-decorated cups, each highlighting flora and fauna of a lunar month. A brief poem was inscribed on the back of each cup. Fewer than ten complete sets of these cups dating to the Kangxi reign are known to exist, and one set was auctioned recently for $2.5 million. I had access to photographs (not very detailed) of two sets, and English paraphrases of the poems from two sets, and from this material I was able to adapt, expand, and imagine the cups and place them in the hands of the Emperor during some imaginary strolls around the palace grounds. I have described the actual tree blossoms, flowers, plants, and animals which are depicted on the cups, a fox-fairy miniature of the Imperial gardens.

These "month" cups are described as wine cups, but I have taken the liberty to make Kangxi exclusively a tea-drinker. His long life and mental acuity seem more in keeping with abstinence from the wine that made fools of so many emperors and generals. After watching Emperor Li Yu (see below) pay the price for his habits, I found Kangxi more akin to my own tea preferences.

Emperor Li Yu, A Life in Poems

I published *Emperor Li Yu, A Life in Poems* as a separate book in late 2022. The hardcover edition includes the Chinese originals of all the poems, and lavish full-bleed illustrations taken from Chinese paintings. The English text presented here is identical, the photos reproduced in grayscale.

For much of the tenth century of the current era, there was no single empire that we might call "China." The great Tang Dynasty, after almost two hundred years of rule over many provinces, collapsed in 907 CE. The period that follows is called by historians, maddeningly, "Five Dynasties and Ten Kingdoms."

Because the Northern and Southern Song dynasties that contended in this era, prevailed militarily and culturally, the Song Dynasty is generally listed as the successor to Tang.

One lingering kingdom, however, the Southern Tang, attracts our attention as it held out under three generations of the Li family of kings. In 937 CE, the Lis replaced the Emperor of Wu and declared themselves the true successors to Tang. From its capital in Nanjing, "Southern Tang" extended its control to six provinces by 951 CE.

Ten years later, the young Li Yu inherited the throne, and it was all downhill from there, at least from the perspective of historians whose focus is territorial conquest. Expansion had already ceased, and territories had been lost to rival states. Worst of all, the new Song Empire threatened invasion, and took Li Yu's brother, sent as a negotiator, as hostage. No matter what Li Yu called himself, or by what title his people addressed him, he slid from emperor to king by imperceptible steps. Yet every king wished himself to be emperor, and as fortunes waxed and waned, no one knew who would prevail.

The man I shall persist in calling "Emperor" Li Yu, was held in contempt by his own officials, and by most historians, for his utter disinterest in military affairs. He would not invade his neighbors, and refused plans that would have acted in a pre-emptive manner against the ever-aggressive Song.

Li Yu is portrayed as dissolute, a man fond of wine, who dallied with concubines and carried on an affair with his Empress's young sister, who had probably been brought to court as a lady-in-waiting. She may have been only fourteen when she attracted the emperor's attention.

Looking at Li Yu from a wider vantage, we can see that Li Yu and his empress were devout Buddhists, and that his politics may have been an intentional, if ultimately ineffectual, pacifism. He was popular among the people, and devoted large amounts of the state's dwindling resources to building new Buddhist temples and monasteries. Where many other emperors had been corrupted by the power-lust of generals and court eunuchs, Li Yu, high-minded, chose art and culture as weapons. When the Song emperor demanded that he travel and submit to him at his court, Li Yu refused to go, and sent emissaries with poetry and art.

His devotion to the arts extended to constructing a pavilion as a home for poets and artists who fled from war-torn neighboring states. Southern Tang thus had a Camelot-like atmosphere. Painting, poetry, and calligraphy were all one continuum, spilling over into architecture, ceramics and bronze works, many now priceless treasures.

Chinese poetry, already ancient, was a vast puzzle-work of allusion, not only to nature and the well-known symbols of Chinese art and mythology, but also to the vast literature that already existed. Everyone wrote poems, and everyone could cite great poems of the past.

Li's poems — of which only 39 survive — are examples of a then-new form called *ci*, in which the form and shape of a poem paralleled a musical melody. The Empress Zhou, an accomplished musician, composed many of the melodies from which the poems take their names.

Although Li Yu's poems begin with an atmosphere of care-free contemplation, domestic tragedies darken his work. The death of a beloved child, and then the passing of his Empress, mark him as a man no longer capable of simple joy. His forbidden affair with his wife's sister is a sensual counterpoint, and when he resolves to make the young woman his second empress, that provides only a brief interval of contentment.

Soon all was swept away when Li Yu was captured after a long siege of his capital. He was at a Buddhist shrine composing a poem when enemy soldiers seized him.

For two years, Li Yu and a few members of his family and court, languished in exile. His palaces had been looted, his court dispersed. As a royal captive, he was treated well, and seems to have been put on show at banquets by the Song emperor as proof of his conquest. Li Yu seems to have accepted this humiliation.

The poems that Li Yu composed in exile may be the saddest short lyrics ever written. Some of the home-sick verses deeply offended the Song Emperor, who then raped Li Yu's young empress. The final humiliation, according to tradition, came when a banquet was offered up in Li

Yu's "honor" and his captor sent a vessel of poisoned wine to the table, which Li Yu was compelled to drink.

Li Yu died in the year 978 CE in his fortieth year. With his murder, the dream of Southern Tang, and its peaceable kingdom, perished.

Li Yu's poems are classics of Chinese literature, and one or more of them appear in many anthologies of Chinese poetry. Surprisingly, there has only been one book presenting all of his poems in English. This was done as literal translations, rendered in elegant English, in 1948, by Liu Yih-Ling (1903-1994), a Chinese scholar, teacher and calligrapher, jointly with the Bengali poet Hasan Shaheed Suhrawardy (1890-1965), and published without copyright in Calcutta. I suspect that the collaboration relied upon Liu's literal version of the Chinese poems and their context, and Suhrawardy's substantial skills as an English-language poet. Suhrawardy was a modernist poet, a friend of D. H. Lawrence and other British writers, and a writer and BBC radio lecturer on Asian art. The book, using one of Li Yu's other honorifics, was titled *Poems of Lee Hou-chu*. Although I have seen this volume dismissed with contempt by at least one academic, I have shown it to several Chinese-speaking friends and asked them about specific points in the poems, and in each case the English was not found wanting. I have examined a few online pages devoted to Li Yu's poems and found nothing there to enlighten me further.

In any case, this cycle of poems is *not* a literal translation, so China scholars may dismiss my effort out of hand if they wish. Using the same method I have employed with poets in other languages, I present here my adaptation and expansion from Li Yu's poems, in which I delineate Li Yu's personal story. Poems are now associated with Li Yu, Empress Zhou, and her younger sister. They are pinned to specific events. New poems are invented and added to advance the narrative. And finally, I end the cycle assuming Li Yu's voice and imagine him writing a final poem while dying of poison, saying all the last things that needed to be said. It also serves as epilogue tying together all the preceding poems.

I have invented titles for all the poems. The original "titles" in Chinese are simply the names of the songs on which the poems were based metrically; as a result, several Li Yu poems have the same title. The Chinese titles in any case have nothing to do with the contents.

These works were written over a period of about three weeks in summer 2022, except for three which I had adapted in 2013. They are free-verse improvisations, in which every line of Li Yu's poems are enveloped in a larger framework. Some of the elaborations spell out Chinese traditions and ideas, such as the festival description in "Sweeping the Tombs," or the themes associated with the parasol tree. Now and then, perhaps, Li Yu utters a philosophical line that is more Greek than Buddhist, but that was unavoidable as I let the character of Li Yu inhabit me and came to trust the voice in which he spoke.

I do a lot of writing in blank verse, and I could well have revised my rhapsodic short-line verse into a more formal meter, but I found that I was content to let these lines roll down the page just as they first came to me.

ABOUT THIS BOOK

The body type of this book is set in 12-point Plantin. Small titles are set in Morris Golden, a font created by William Morris for the Kelmscott Press in 1890. This modern digital recreation of the type by the P22 Type Foundry simulates the soft-edged impression of hand-set metal type on hand-made paper. Morris in turn based his designs on typefaces created by Nicolas Jenson. Larger titles are set in Solemnis, an uncial-style font designed by Günter Gerhard Lange in 1953. Lange created many classic revival fonts for the Berthold foundry, leading that organization through the eras of metal, photo and then digital type design.

The book has been illustrated with digitally-edited and enhanced images principally taken from classic Chinese hand-scrolls and paintings, most of them from the Tang and Song dynasties. The images are placed to suggest the persons, places, and atmosphere of the surrounding poems; none are actual portrayals of Li Yu or his family. Tang and Song art often present imaginary and idealized landscapes and fantastic architecture, so these have stood in for palace views.

"Bai Hu, The White Tiger" and "October Storm" first appeared in *Anniversarius: The Book of Autumn* (2011). "Old Scholar Under Autumn Trees" first appeared in *The Inhuman Wave* (2020). "On a Chinese Fan" and "The Loft on Fourteenth Street" appeared in *An Expectation of Presences* (2012). *Li Yu, A Life in Poems* was published as a bilingual hardcover edition in 2022. Earlier drafts of "Down South," "Pretending to Be A Fisherman," "Meditation in Exile," and "The Beloved Speaks" appeared as "Four Poems of Li Yu" in *Trilobite Love Song* (2014).

ABOUT THE AUTHOR

American neo-Romantic poet Brett Rutherford, born in Scottdale, PA, began writing poetry seriously in his 15th year. His first poems were in Latin. During his twenties he lived in New York City, San Francisco, and at the glacial lake in Edinboro, PA where he attended college. He founded The Poet's Press in New York City in 1971, and the press still operates today with more than 300 titles produced. He returned to his native state in 2016, residing in Squirrel Hill in Pittsburgh.

Most of his middle years were divided between New York and New England. After a literary pilgrimage to Providence, RI, on the track of H. P. Lovecraft and Edgar Allan Poe, he moved there with his press in 1985. Several moves back and forth from New York City, Weehawken NJ on the cliffs overlooking Manhattan, and Boston, found him again in Providence, where he returned to college at University of Rhode Island. After finishing his master's degree, he worked there in distance learning, and taught several courses for the Gender and Women's Studies Program. In Pittsburgh, he has taught at the University of Pittsburgh's OSHER adult education program.

In addition to his many volumes of his own poetry, Rutherford has turned his attention in recent years to adaptations and translations from Russian, German, French, Spanish, Latin, and Greek poets and writers. He sees this as a continuation of the kind of cross-cultural poetic work done by American poets like Longfellow in the 19th century.

He has also prepared annotated editions of Matthew Gregory Lewis's *Tales of Wonder*, the poetry of Charles Hamilton Sorley, the poetry and criticism of Sarah Helen Whitman, and the collected writings of Emilie Glen and Barbara A. Holland.

Made in the USA
Middletown, DE
26 March 2023

26989232R00116